The
EQUIP
Series

The Gospel, the Church, and Homosexuality

How the Gospel is Still the Power of God
for Redemption and Transformation

Edited by
Michael Sanelli
and
Derek Brown

GBF Press
Sunnyvale, CA

The Gospel, the Church, and Homosexuality

The Gospel, the Church, and Homosexuality
Copyright © 2018 Michael Sanelli and Derek Brown

Published by GBF Press.

For more titles, please visit our website at GBFPress.com.

Requests for information about GBF PRESS can be sent to:

GBFPress@gbfsv.org

All rights reserved.

ISBN-13: 978-0692044933
ISBN-10: 0692044930

Scripture quotations are from the ESV® Bible (The Holy Bible, English Standard Version®), copyright © 2001 by Crossway, a publishing ministry of Good News Publishers. Used by permission. All rights reserved.

Cover Design: Lauren Carter
Cover Production: Bob Douglas

This work is a publication of GBF Press. No part of this publication may be reproduced, stored in a retrieval system, or transmitted in any form or by any means except by permission of the publisher.

Dedicated to the Saints at
Grace Bible Church, Pleasant Hill, California;
Grace Bible Fellowship, Sunnyvale, California; and
Calvary Community Church, Knightsen, California.

Contents

	Acknowledgments	ix
1	**Introduction:** Cultivating a Gospel Culture in the Local Church *Michael Sanelli*	9
2	**The Gospel and Homosexuality:** The Power of God for Genuine Transformation *Ryan Rippee*	21
3	**Living Together in the Hope of the Gospel:** How Shall the Church Respond to Those Struggling with Same-Sex Attraction? *Scott Denny*	49
4	**Truth with Kindness:** Sharing the Gospel with the Homosexual Community *Derek Brown*	69
5	**Something Good, and Something Even Better:** A Biblical Vision of Human Sexuality *Derek Brown*	97
6	**Conclusion:** Changing Nation, Unchanging Mission *Derek Brown*	121
	Notes	131
	Scripture Index	137
	Recommended Resources	143
	About the Authors	145

Acknowledgments

We are grateful for the church of Jesus Christ! It is for the church we write, and it is in the church that we have found many willing servants to help with this important project. Special thanks goes to Scott Denny and Ryan Rippee for their contributions to this volume. We would also like to thank Cliff McManis and Breanna Paniagua for their help during the editing process. Thank you to Jasmine Patton for her helpful edits and for creating the Scripture index. We pray that this book will be helpful to you as you think through this important topic and minister to your friends and family.

For Christ and his Church,

Michael Sanelli
Derek Brown
Pleasant Hill, California
February 8, 2018

1

Introduction
Cultivating a Gospel Culture in the Local Church

Michael Sanelli

Introduction

Al Mohler recently wrote, "The 20th century will be recognized as the century of the greatest change in sexual morality in the history of Western civilization."[1] Only time will tell whether or not this will be so. However, it is true that we are living in a time of an unprecedented sexual revolution. It is no wonder why so many Christian leaders have sought to bring biblical clarity to these issues. Gender identity, human sexuality, and the LGBT community have been the topic of endless books, articles, sermons, blogs, vlogs, and Tweets.

The primary goal of this contribution is not to exegetically argue for the biblical view of homosexuality in any great detail—although, we are of the conviction that homosexual practice is not affirmed by the Scriptures. Many detailed and well-written books exist by better theologians and authors who have demonstrated this as the stance of both the historical church and the Bible.[2]

So, if the aim of our book is not to delineate our position on homosexuality, what is the aim?

The Problem We Hope to Address

The book you hold in your hands is the product of a conference we held in the summer of 2016 identically designated *The Gospel, The Church and Homosexuality*. Prior to the conference I got together with the authors of this book on a few occasions–both digitally and physically–to discuss what I had been praying would be a fruitful day of preaching and discussion.

It has been our goal to see God's people align their hearts to that of Christ's towards those who struggle with same-sex attraction in our churches and those who identify with the LGBT community. Beyond mastering the biblical reasons why homosexual behavior is sinful, God's people ought to bare Christ's heart of compassion. Doesn't the gospel compel us to do so?

Paul wrote to the Roman church, "For I am not ashamed of the gospel, for it is the power of God for salvation to everyone who believes" (Rom 1:16). Does the church still believe this verse? Is the gospel powerful enough to bring about salvation—from beginning to the end—for anyone and everyone? Is faith in the gospel truly the "power of God" to thoroughly transform sinful, rebellious hearts and unite them to the only mediator and Savior, Jesus Christ? Most evangelicals would undoubtedly respond with a resounding, "Yes!" However, I wonder if we have only believed this in theory.

Christian leaders have given an array of responses on this topic to the church and to the watching society. At one extreme, there are those who completely affirm homosexual behavior, claiming the Bible fully supports the LGBT community in their sexual practices.[3] The heart underlying this position hopefully comes from a desire for inclusivity—to love the LGBT community—which is commendable. They do so, however, at the expense of the clear teaching and authority of Scripture. Perhaps, in some way, they have also forgotten that the gospel is the power of God for redemption and transformation—a holistic salvation. If the gospel doesn't have the power to transform a sinner's heart, maybe we need to transform the meaning of sin. If the Bible's answer to the homosexual community is offensive, maybe we need change the Bible's answer.

At the other extreme, there are those who have not only condemned homosexual behavior, noting that the Bible clearly identifies the behavior as sin, but who have also filled their response with hate, using inflammatory statements like, "God hates fags."[4]

These responses we find to be repulsive. Not only does this sort of hate speech cloud the realities of the gospel, it drags the name of Jesus down into the filth of self-righteousness, gross bigotry, and malice. Though they may uphold the Bible's authority, they too have forgotten that the gospel is the power of God to transform hearts. Can those who identify as homosexual be transformed by the gospel? Paul, inspired and filled by the Holy Spirit, seems to think so (1 Cor 6:9-10).

These are both extreme responses within evangelicalism. Most gospel-preaching, Bible-believing churches would agree that we must uphold the Bible's position that homosexual behavior is a sin and that the gospel is available to anyone who believes, whether from among the LGBT community or not. They would also have a similar repulsion to the hate speech of Westboro Baptist Church.

The problem isn't so much our answer to the question of whether or not homosexuality is a sin. The problem is that the evangelical church has too often left it at that. Conservative Bible believers have more often than not preached the *bad news* in their responses to the culture regarding homosexuality without getting to the *good news* of the gospel. We are proficient at communicating that homosexuality is a sin. Why wouldn't the LGBT community keep themselves at arm's length from the doors of our churches if this is all we tell them?

The Gospel, the Church, and Homosexuality

The fruit of this kind of gospel negligence doesn't only affect the LGBT community outside our church walls; it affects those who struggle against homosexual desires within our church communities. By and large it seems that the evangelical church has responded poorly to the pain experienced by those who identify as homosexual and those within our churches that experience same-sex attraction (SSA). In fact, in many ways, it appears that our general responses have only increased their pain and the feeling of rejection by the church.

Rather than communicating the gospel and seasoning our responses with grace, the church more often has been the voice of indictment and condemnation. Whether or not all of society's accusations of Christianity are true of our own churches, it would be incumbent upon the church to be "quick to hear, slow to speak, and slow to anger" (James 1:19). This is especially true in our conversations with and regarding the LGBT community, as well as what we say about homosexual desire in general.

Do we demonstrate with our words and actions to those in our churches who struggle with SSA and to the members of the LGBT community that we believe the gospel is the power of God for salvation? Or, have we communicated that their sins are unforgivable, an abomination, disgusting, or simply something worth joking about? It's no wonder those who struggle amongst us keep silent or leave our churches altogether. It's no wonder the LGBT community seems to think that the Christian church hates them. When someone within our church struggles with same-sex desire and all they hear about the subject are either jokes or condemnation, they may begin to believe the lie that the gospel isn't God's power for them or people like them.

What we long to see in our churches and in yours is a culture that is so saturated with the gospel that anyone who struggles with any sinful desire would feel comfortable to be open, know that they are loved and cared for, and experience the transforming power of the gospel.

The Gospel Culture We Hope to Stimulate

We need to begin seeing this as more than an issue to be addressed or a topic on which to speak. As Preston Sprinkle observes, "Homosexuality is not an issue to be solved; it's about people who need to love and be loved."[5] How can we create a culture in which this is possible in our churches? How can we be a church who so loves the gospel that this kind of love is felt by those among us who struggle with SSA and is even felt by the onlooking LGBT community?

I have a confession to make that I hope will illustrate the kind of repentance I hope this book will promote. I recall a specific moment when the Holy Spirit, through the preaching of the Word, convicted me of my sin of self-righteousness, which was often displayed in hypocrisy and a judgmental spirit. I believe I was in high school at the time. I do not remember most of the circumstances surrounding the situation—which church was I attending, who was preaching, and so on. But at one point the preacher brought up the well-known passage about the prideful Pharisee and the penitent sinner in Luke 18:9-14.

> "[Jesus] also told this parable to some who trusted in themselves that they were righteous, and treated others with contempt: "Two men went up into the temple to pray, one a Pharisee and the other a tax collector. The Pharisee, standing by himself, prayed thus: 'God, I thank you that I am not like other men, extortioners, unjust, adulterers, or even like this tax collector. I fast twice a week; I give tithes of all that I get.' But the tax collector, standing far off, would not even lift up his eyes to heaven, but beat his breast, saying, 'God, be merciful to me, a sinner!' I tell you, this man went down to his house justified, rather than the other. For everyone who exalts himself will be humbled, but the one who humbles himself will be exalted."

I found myself in that very moment thinking, "Wow. What a prideful man that Pharisee was. He didn't really get the gospel. He thought his standing before the Lord was based on his works, not on Christ. I'm glad I'm not so blindly prideful and judgmental as that Pharisee was…" Just then the Spirit approached me just as Nathan did to King David saying, "You are that man." I remember sitting there stone-faced trying to keep my composure. My problem was that I hadn't let the gospel dictate the way I saw other people's sin; only my own. This sort of attitude and mindset in our churches suppresses a gospel culture and silences people in their struggles.

Let's create a culture where the Pharisees' prayers are confronted and open humility is welcomed. Maybe then we can be a gospel-illumined beacon to those who struggle in our churches and to the LGBT community.

A Gospel Community

Faith in the gospel of Jesus Christ not only has the power to transform individuals, but also to create a gospel community. The gospel "is the power of God for salvation to everyone who believes" (Romans 1:16) and upon believing, that individual is not only united to Christ but also to Christ's body, the church, for "we, though many, are one body in Christ, and individually members of one another" (Romans 12:5).

What is needed is a gospel culture in that gospel-created community. It's not enough for us to say we believe the tenets of the gospel; the gospel must give shape to the very culture of our churches. Ray Ortlund Jr. defines gospel culture in this way: it is the "shared experience of grace for the undeserving: the corporate incarnation of the biblical message in the relationships, vibe, feel, tone, values, priorities, aroma, honesty, freedom, gentleness, humility, cheerfulness—indeed, the total human reality of a church defined and sweetened by the gospel."[6]

In our purpose statements, core values, and doctrinal statements, we declare that genuine faith in Christ crucified is the means to this salvation, the forgiveness of *all* your trespasses. We say the gospel puts us all in the same place: the ground is level at the foot of the cross. We all stand before the living God only by the merit of Christ, as debtors to mercy. The question is this: do we believe this to be true about the gospel on paper but not in practice? Does gospel doctrine truly inform our church culture?

This isn't a matter of only believing the gospel individually. It's what a local church should look and feel like if it truly has believed the gospel. If we've all undeservingly received grace, where is there room for boasting or considering one sinner as less important than another (see Rom 3:27-31; 1 Cor 4:7)? If we've all been forgiven so much, how can we act as though one person's sin is stranger or more taboo than another? If the gospel has so powerfully transformed us all, how can we act as though Christ cannot help those who struggle with one sin but not another?

This gospel culture can be summarized in a helpful equation from Ortlund's book *The Gospel: How the Church Portrays the Beauty of Christ*.

> I think of it with a simple equation: gospel + safety + time. The family of God is where people should find lots of gospel, lots of safety, and lots of time. In other words, the people in our churches need:
>
> - multiple exposures to the happy news of the gospel from one end of the Bible to the other;
>
> - the safety of non-accusing sympathy so that they can admit their problems honestly; and
>
> - enough time to rethink their lives at a deep level, because people are complex and changing is not easy.[7]

It's hard for people to feel safe enough to share their struggle with pornography, cheating, and lying. But how much more difficult can it be for those who struggle with SSA when we are not purposeful to create this kind of environment for them? Speaking about same-sex attraction in the church, Christopher Yuan, a Christian who once identified with the LGBT community, said this in a talk at the 2015 The Gospel Coalition National Conference: "Do you know how hard it is to open up to another Christian, even a pastor, about this issue of sexuality? It can be one of the…scariest things…to do."[8]

Where We're Headed
I've only scratched the surface on the implications of the gospel for our churches. Chapter 2 will further explore the connection we must make with the gospel and individuals who identify with the LGBT community and individuals suffering in our local churches. There we will examine more ways in which the gospel ought to inform our relationships with one another and our thoughts on homosexuality.

In Chapter 3, we seek to specifically implore the church to come alongside those in our congregations who struggle with SSA with the hope of the gospel. When someone shares with you that they are struggling with SSA, how will you respond and what hope can you give them?

At this point you may ask, How then shall we approach the LGBT community with the gospel? If I understand that I need to see this issue through the lens of the gospel and that I can give gospel hope to those inside our church walls, how do I then extend the gospel of grace to those outside the church? We will explore this question in Chapter 4.

Finally, in Chapter 5 we consider the biblical understanding of human sexuality. What are God's good purposes for sexual expression, and how to we communicate these purposes in such a sexually saturated society? If homosexuality isn't God's design for human sexual expression, what is, and why?

Our Prayer for You

It is my prayer that as you read this book, whether you struggle with same-sex attraction or not, you would rethink your approach to the topic of homosexuality. I pray that you will begin to see those in your churches who struggle with SSA with new eyes of compassion as Christ sees them. May you continue to pray about your interactions with the LGBT community and begin to see with new eyes the hurting and marginalized members of the American population.

If you have somehow missed how the gospel applies to homosexuality, I pray that the Spirit of God would make it clear to you that how you speak about homosexuality, and how you interact with those who struggle with it are not a mere matters of theological nuance, but implications of the gospel itself. May the Lord grant you the grace needed to see how the gospel must inform your church and your perspective on homosexuality.

2

The Gospel and Homosexuality
The Power of God for Genuine Transformation

Ryan Rippee

Historically, the church has not responded well when speaking to the issue of homosexuality. Often we have offered responses that, if they are not outright unbiblical, are certainly less than gospel answers. First, we become judgmental and we condemn with no offer of hope. We may tell someone who pursues homosexual activity that they are in sin, but we do not extend friendship, a loving hand of help, or any good news that Jesus came to seek and save the lost (Luke 19:10).

A second response is that we move away or isolate ourselves from the issue, pretending that it doesn't even exist. This latter approach is the more common way of dealing with homosexuality, particularly as we related with those in the church who struggle with same-sex attraction. Much like how our culture deals with the sick and dying—moving them into hospitals and rest homes that are out of sight and out of mind—we refuse to talk about the issue so that we do not have to deal with it.

The third response is to reduce or re-categorize the issue as something other than a gospel issue. We soon become defined by what we are against and whom we oppose, and, as a result, the good news is lost. Homosexuality becomes merely a political agenda rather than a concern for people made in the image of God who are struggling with sinful desires and actions. Furthermore, in response to what we see in our culture and on the news, we can sin with our tongue by making slanderous remarks that do not reflect Jesus' command to love our neighbor (Matt 22:39).

It really does go back to that statement about loving our neighbor. But who is our neighbor? Can someone within the church struggling with same-sex attraction or even someone outside the church who considers themselves homosexual really be our neighbor? Yes! And we can love them while holding fast to the gospel.

Why Christians Respond Unbiblically to Homosexuality

Why then, do Christians have unbiblical responses towards those who consider themselves homosexual? In his book, *Love into Light: The Gospel, the Homosexual, and the Church*, Peter Hubbard gives four possibilities why we respond unbiblically. First, he says we take on a mindset that (1) "Homosexuals are not like us: they are 'abnormal'"; (2) "Homosexuals have turned aside: their sin is 'unnatural'"; (3) "Homosexuals have a particular identity"; and (4) "Homosexuals are who they are: they will not change."[1]

Growing up, that is exactly how I felt. I believed that those with homosexual desires were abnormal, unnatural, and could never change. However, two events in my twenties caused me to reevaluate my thinking. The first was when I began working at UC Davis in a computer job, and my co-worker identified as homosexual. He kept it hidden, so I worked with him for a year and didn't even know this about him. But then he put pictures at his desk of him and another man together on vacation. In my naiveté at twenty years old I thought to myself, "Oh, wow! You went with your friend on this vacation — that's great!" When he explained to me that this was his lover, I was stunned. Here was someone with whom I'd spent nearly every day of the week over the course of a year, who was a really nice guy, and with whom I had a lot in common. What was going to happen to our relationship?

The second experience happened a number of years later while I was leading a college ministry in Napa. I had two young men in my ministry who came to me and shared their struggles with same-sex attraction, asking how they could escape this temptation. I did not know what to do—or even how to respond—because I thought homosexuals were abnormal. But as I discipled these men over a period of years and began to ask the question, "How do I apply the gospel to this situation?" I repented of my own sin and saw that I needed the gospel just as much as my friends who were battling homosexual desires.

Transforming our Responses with the Gospel

Hubbard, after giving these four examples of unbiblical thinking, rewords the statements in light of the gospel. To the idea that homosexuals are not normal, he says the gospel teaches we are all created in God's image, and after the Fall, all of us are "marred image-bearers."[2] We should not be singling out same-sex attracted people as if their experiences are somehow more repugnant than everyone else's experience of living with a sinful nature. To the second issue that they've turned aside and their sin is unnatural, the gospel says that all have turned aside, and "all sin is twisted" (cf. Rom 3:23; Eph 2:3).[3]

To the third, that homosexuals have a particular identity, the gospel proclaims that all can "find a new identity" in Christ.[4] Those engaged in homosexual practice have embraced an identity of "This is who I am," and some believers have even embraced the title "Gay Christian" as a mark of their identity. But the gospel teaches that our activity doesn't determine our identity; rather, *our identity determines our activity*. Therefore, when someone becomes a Christian, they receive a new identity in Christ, and they are no longer identified by their sinful behaviors.

Finally, to the belief that homosexuals will not change, Hubbard responds with the gospel, which says, "homosexuals and heterosexuals hope in grace together."[5] If you are a Christian, there is great hope because your Father has not left you alone in your struggles. You have been given the Holy Spirit so that, in the New Covenant, you are born again to a living hope (Jer 31:33-34; 1 Pet 1:3). This theology of regeneration means that in Christ you are a new creation (2 Cor 5:17). You have new desires, new affections, and new pursuits so that you are now able to *become* holy. God is remaking his image in you by the Spirit (Col 3:10). Because we all have this same hope, by God's grace, we desire that the world behold the image of God being remade in us. As Paul wrote to the Philippians, "And I am sure of this, that he who began a good work in you will bring it to completion at the day of Jesus Christ" (Phil 1:6).[6]

Terminology

Before we examine how 1 Corinthians 6:9–11 applies the gospel to homosexuality, I want to define some terms and distill them into three categories.

Same-Sex Attraction

The first phrase is "same-sex attraction." Same-sex attraction is the "experience of realizing that you find members of the same gender attractive to the point that you are aroused and romantically captivated."[7] Same-sex attraction is at the level of what the Bible calls "desires," and is the root from which same-sex behavior is the fruit. Through the gospel, the Spirit of God can transform both desires *and* behavior.

In his epistle, James says "Let no one say when he is tempted, 'I am being tempted by God,' for God cannot be tempted with evil, and he himself tempts no one. But each person is tempted when he is lured and enticed by his own desire. Then desire when it has conceived gives birth to sin, and sin when it is fully grown brings forth death" (James 1:13-15). Scripture tells us that the pattern from temptation to sin is the following: each one of us is tempted when they are carried away and enticed by their own desires and lusts. These desires flow out of the heart, and when we are carried away and enticed by these desires, we give into temptation. What a picture! James says that when desires are carried to full term, it is like giving birth to sin, which brings forth death.

Within the theological literature on same-sex attraction, some argue that same-sex attraction is not always just about the sex act. It is not always about being aroused and wanting to have sex with somebody of the same gender. In fact, they have appealed to the bonds of affection between David and Jonathan or Jesus and John to show some sort of biblical same-sex attraction. However, I would respond that if a same-sex relationship does not contain the sexual possibility of arousal and romantic captivation with the possibility of sex, then the biblical term is "friendship." Both David and Jonathan, as well as Jesus and his disciples, are examples of "a friend who sticks closer than a brother" (Prov 18:24; cf. John 15:15). These are examples of deep and abiding spiritual friendship.

The Gospel, the Church, and Homosexuality

If you desire affection and emotion with someone of the same gender, without sexual attraction, that is not same-sex attraction or same-sex orientation, but friendship. And Scripture teaches that friendship a *good* desire. However, our culture is broken and misguided on this issue, and it often teaches young men that all they *are* is their sexuality. The porn industry, popular entertainment, retail marketing, and their ever-present availability online, aim to reduce men to nothing more than their sexual desire. For the young women, much of the culture wants to reduce them to their body image, using all the same avenues to create the ideal of a woman that, in reality, does not exist.

But Scripture teaches that both men and women are created in the image of God and created for meaningful relationships. Before He created anything, the Triune God has existed in relationship from eternity past. The Father, Son, and Spirit have been living in a perfect, intimate, loving community for all eternity. It is a good thing, therefore, as God's image-bearers, to desire deep and intimate relationships. Furthermore, the church is the showcase of God's work of renewing all things in Christ by the Spirit—including relationships—and is therefore the best community someone can join.

Kevin DeYoung recalls a statement from a friend that,

> same-sex attraction—used here to mean more than men simply desiring the company of other men or women—did not exist

> before the fall, comes as a result of it, and will not exist when the fall has been finally overcome. Desires are deemed good or bad, not just by their intensity or their sense of proportion, but based upon their object."[8]

Therefore, as we move through this chapter, it is important to remember that our desires are good or bad based upon the object of those desires.

Gay-Identity

The second phrase that I want to define is "gay identity." If attraction is about what I *feel*, then identity is about *who* I am. And because identity is a matter of choice, it is also a moral responsibility. Sam Allberry's description of his own experience is helpful. "The kind of sexual attractions I experienced," he writes, "are not fundamental to my identity. They are a part of *what I feel* but they're not *who I am* in a fundamental sense. I am far more than my sexuality."[9] He later reflects, "Desires for things God has forbidden are a reflection of how sin has distorted me, not how God has made me."[10] Likewise, Rosaria Butterfield stresses,

> There is no ontological category of sexual orientation. The idea of identity emerging from sexual desire embodies a philosophy of the soul that is false. . . . Christians who feel beholden by culture to use the concept of sexual orientation ought to stop and ask one question: where ought we to situate sexual

> orientation in relation to biblical principles? If we were to fish around for a biblical place to contain this neologism (which is sloppy theology at best), it could only be traced to the biblical concept of "flesh."[11]

Butterfield is placing "gay identity" into the biblical category of the flesh, and Christians "are not in the flesh but in the Spirit" (Rom 8:9).

Homosexual Behavior

The third phrase I want to define is "homosexual behavior." Homosexual behavior is the choice to engage in sexual practices with or be stimulated by a member of the same gender, and Scripture is very clear that homosexual behavior is sin (1 Cor 6:9; cf. 1 Tim 1:10). However, it is important to remember that we never interact with categories; we interact with people. If we reduce someone to a primary area of struggle in his or her life, we are not being fair, accurate, or helpful.

The Major Concern

In summary, we can say, "Yes, Scripture teaches that homosexual behavior is a sin." Furthermore, because rooting one's identity in a homosexuality orientation is a matter of choice, it is therefore a moral responsibility, and also an issue of sin. But what about same-sex attraction? If it comes out of the desires of the heart, with its object something that did not exist before the fall, and will not exist after the fall—is the attraction itself sin?

I know that in my own struggles with heterosexual desires, for example, that I can be *tempted from without* by a woman walking by on the street who is dressed for summer. According to James, if I am carried away by that desire, I have given birth to sin (James 1:13–15), but the temptation from without is not itself sin. For how else could Jesus be "one who in every respect has been tempted as we are, yet without sin" (Heb 4:15). However, when the temptation is from *within*, arising from our own hearts, Scripture calls them "impurity, passion, evil desire" that we are to "put to death" (Col 3:5; cf. Rom 8:9). For both forms of temptation, the answer is the same. It is the gospel.

What, then, is the major concern for us here? It is the sufficiency of the Word of God, which really means it is the sufficiency of the Lord Jesus Christ. Is Jesus able to save? Is He able to deliver? Is He able to heal? Is He able to change us? If He is, then He is able to work at the level of our affections and desires and give us new ones by the power of the Spirit. Scripture is clear on this. As a pastor, my greatest concern is our conception of the greatness and power of Christ. He is the glorious, all-sufficient Savior who delivers from the bondage and brokenness of sin.

The Danger with Finding an Identity Outside of Christ

In 1 Corinthians 6:9–11, we see the wonderful news regarding the greatness and the power of Christ. Because of the finished work of Jesus, Christians are no longer defined by their sin, but rather by who they are in Him. The specific moral failures in verses 9–11 continue a theme that began in verses 1–8 about not suing a brother or sister. There were those in the church of Corinth that were sacrificing the credibility of their Christian identity for the sake of personal retribution. That is, rather than being more concerned about Christ's reputation in their local community, they were greedy for financial gain. According to this passage, then, there are three dangers of finding an identity outside of Christ: (1) it is characterized by wickedness, (2) it is a matter of self-delusion, and (3) it allows behavior to determine identity.

It is Characterized by Wickedness

Paul writes, "Do you not know the unrighteous will not inherit the kingdom of God" (1 Cor 6:9)? The reason he ties these two subjects together is because he wants the church to see that is how the unrighteous live: they live for personal gratification. The unrighteous take each other to court so that they can get all that their heart desires. Paul then gives a list in verses 9-10 of personal desires, gratified by the flesh, that characterize those who will not inherit the kingdom. In other words, verses 9–10 speak of an identity outside of Christ. Paul's emphasis here is on the habits or dispositions of people who practice evil. When he calls them "unrighteous" (v. 9), he is describing those characterized by wickedness. Because their identity is outside of Christ, God sees them as unrighteous and wicked, which is proven by their behavior. As a result, they will be judged and will not inherit the kingdom of God.

One of my best friends had to wait a long time before God brought him a wife, and I remember his temptation, while he waited to find his identity in marriage. He was tempted to believe the lie that if he could just get married, then he could really live and serve the Lord. However, he learned that a wife was not his answer to being alone. God was his answer to being alone. Now that he is married he has learned that God is also his answer to being married. Similarly, the driving concern of Paul in this passage when he begins to list sexual sins in verses 9-10 is not abstinence or singleness; it is identity. Our identity is far more than our sexuality or our abstinence. Paul's goal is that Christians would live out their identity in Christ and therefore become Christ*like*.

Later in the chapter, Paul writes, "Flee from sexual immorality. Every other sin a person commits is outside the body, but the sexually immoral person sins against his own body" (1 Cor 6:18). Growing up in the church, I cannot count the number of times I was told the underlying threat of this passage is that if you have sex outside of marriage, you will get a sexually transmitted disease, so you better flee sexual temptation just like Joseph.

But the motive for purity is not found in verse 18; it is found in verses 19–20: "Or do you not know that your body is a temple of the Holy Spirit within you, whom you have from God? You are not your own, for you were bought with a price. So glorify God in your body." The motivation for holiness and purity, whether in singleness or marriage, is the gospel. We were bought with a price. The Lord Jesus paid the penalty for our sin. We are not our own; rather, we belong to Him. Therefore, we ought to glorify God in our body. In marriage, purity is seen in fidelity to our mate. In singleness, purity is seen in celibacy. But our desire in each case should be to glorify Christ as our response to the good news. Thus, one danger with seeking an identity outside of Christ is that such a pursuit is characterized by wickedness rather than righteousness and motivated by self-gratification rather than the gospel.

It is a Matter of Self-Delusion

In verse 9, Paul tells the Corinthians, "Do not be deceived." What is the deception? The deception is to think that God will not judge people for their sin. In other words, the reality is that those who find their identity outside of Christ and pursue unrighteous activities will be condemned at the final judgment and will not inherit the kingdom of God, regardless of what they presently profess about their relationship with God. Similarly, in Ephesians 5:5, Paul tells the Ephesian church, "For you may be sure of this, that everyone who is sexually immoral or impure, or who is covetous (that is, an idolater), has no inheritance in the kingdom of Christ and God."

So how are we deceived in this matter? I think it comes when folks use sophisticated arguments to argue that homosexual behavior is approved by God. For example, some argue that the prohibitions against homosexuality are temporary and that they were only in the Old Testament (e.g., Lev 18:22) so they're not for us today. Others argue that the prohibitions against homosexuality are misunderstood; they are only for acts that are sexually violent, like the attempted rape by those in Sodom and Gomorrah (Gen 19:5-11). Still others argue that prohibitions against homosexuality are simply due to ignorance, because they were enforced before scientists discovered the category of sexual orientation. Perhaps as Christians living in our current generation, the greatest deception is to think that since God is loving and forgiving, it must also mean He not only tolerates but approves the homosexual behavior. Therefore, if we disapprove of homosexual behavior, we are unloving and bigoted.

One final deception argues, "God wants me to be happy. I have same-sex attraction, and living and fulfilling my sexuality is the only way I can be happy! God surely doesn't want me to suffer my whole life with this same-sex attraction, say 'no' to it and battle it my whole life."

To be deceived in this manner is to assume that no judgment is coming. Those who live in an identity outside of Christ are self-deluded, but in Christ, holiness and happiness go hand in hand. To the Galatians, Paul writes, "Do not be deceived: God is not mocked, for whatever one sows, that will he also reap. For the one who sows to his own flesh will from the flesh reap corruption, but the one who sows to the Spirit will from the Spirit reap eternal life" (Gal 6:7–8). For the Christian, the experience of same-sex attraction is a form of suffering, but as Paul told the Romans, "we rejoice in our sufferings, knowing that suffering produces endurance, and endurance produces character, and character produces hope, and hope does not put us to shame, because God's love has been poured into our hearts through the Holy Spirit who was given to us" (Rom 5:3–5). True happiness and joy is a Spirit-empowered gift from the Father that enables us to endure the sufferings inherent in sinful sexual desires, because of the hope of eternal life found in Christ.

It is Allowing Behavior to Determine Identity

After Paul tells the Corinthians not to be deceived, he gives a list of those who will not inherit the kingdom of God: "the sexually immoral, nor idolaters, nor adulterers, nor men who practice homosexuality, nor thieves, nor the greedy, nor drunkards, nor revilers, nor swindlers" (1 Cor 6:9–10). Essentially, he is teaching that those who live in an identity outside of Christ are allowing their behavior to determine their identity.

The phrase "nor men who practice homosexuality" actually translates two words in the Greek, *malakoi* (literally, "soft") and *arsenokoites* (literally, "someone who sleeps with other males"). From the historical evidence, Paul apparently coined the latter term in reference to

Leviticus 18:22 and 20:13, where the Old Testament prohibits homosexual behavior. Kevin DeYoung writes about the importance of this phrase for our contemporary discussion:

> If Paul wanted his readers to know he was referring only to exploitative forms of homosexuality, he wouldn't have coined a term from a portion of the Mosaic law where all sex involving a man with a man is forbidden. Was Paul opposed only to exploitative forms of incest in 1 Corinthians 5? Was he telling those Christians entangled in sexual immorality to flee only from exploitative forms of adultery, fornication, and prostitution in the second half of 1 Corinthians 6? Are we really to suppose that Paul— just after urging excommunication for sexual sin (5:4–5, 13), and just as he references the Mosaic law (6:9), and just before he anchors his sexual ethic in the Genesis creation story (6:16) — meant to say, "Obviously, I'm not talking about two adult men in a long-term relationship"? And if he had meant to communicate such a message to the Corinthians or to Timothy [*arsenokoites* use in 1 Tim. 1:10], how would that have been obvious to any of them?[12]

The Gospel, the Church, and Homosexuality

It is important to remember that in this context, homosexual sin is not unique. Paul's list includes other forms of sexual sin (sexual immorality and adultery), and his list includes non-sexual forms of sin (theft, greed, drunkenness, abusive people, swindlers). Paul teaches that God will judge it all, so to speak up about the dangers of finding one's identity outside of Christ is actually a loving act. If we were to speak the truth to someone and say, "Hey, listen, if you're a thief, you're not going to inherit the kingdom of God. If you engage in a lifestyle of stealing from people, you're not going to inherit the kingdom of God and you need to stop stealing and turn to Christ," we would conclude it is a loving thing to do. So it is with homosexual sin. Sam Allberry comments,

> Homosexual sin is serious. Paul says that the active and unrepentant homosexual (as with all the unrighteous) will not enter God's kingdom. This is a very stark truth. Paul also reminds his readers not to be deceived on this point. He assumes there will be those who deny this teaching, and argue that some forms of homosexual conduct are acceptable to God. But Paul is clear: homosexual conduct leads people to destruction. To teach otherwise (as a number of purportedly Christian leaders sadly do) is tantamount to sending people to hell. This is a gospel issue.[13]

On June 13, 2016, I woke up to the news that the night before (June 12), a shooting occurred at the Pulse nightclub in Orlando, Florida, in which 49 people were killed and 53 wounded. The first thing I did at our church service was to pray corporately for the victims and their families and friends. As I prayed, I did not explain that the shooting was at a gay bar, nor did I speak ill of their behavior. I simply prayed that God would use this evil act to bring the gospel into their community. Of course, I knew that my church would read the news and understand the background. My greatest concern was to model to my flock that all sinful behavior, whether heterosexual or homosexual, finds its remedy in the gospel. Since Christ is sufficient for all, I was determined to model prayer that would be the same for anyone who was lost apart from Christ.

Jesus was a friend of tax collectors and sinners, but it wasn't their behavior that He affirmed. Rather, it was their humanity he affirmed and the fact that they are made in the image of God. We need to learn from Jesus at this point. We need to learn how to love our neighbor and, without affirming their behavior, speak the truth in love to those who not only experience same-sex attraction, but who are presently engaging in homosexual activity. In fact, we need to warn them of the danger of allowing their behavior to determine their identity: they will not inherit the kingdom of God.

The Joy of Finding Our Identity in Christ

Paul comes to the wonderful news of the gospel in verse 11. For those who have found their identity in Christ, he says, "Such were some of you." Paul is not saying that we are no longer tempted by the sins he listed in the previous verses. Those of us who have been saved for any amount of time know that we can still be tempted by what we did in our pre-Christian lifestyle. What Paul is saying is that we are no longer *defined* by these things. If you were a thief before coming to Christ, you are no longer known as a thief. If you were an adulterer before believing the gospel, you no long bear that scarlet letter. Rather, you are known as a child of God, a Christian, a follower of Jesus. "Such were some of you." Instead of our activity determining our identity, now our identity determines our activity. Paul then unpacks three realities inherent to this new identity: (1) being "washed" clean; (2) being "sanctified; and (3) being "justified."

Washed Clean

Paul first speaks of Christians as those who were "washed clean." This washing is a picture of Spirit baptism, of which physical baptism is a sign (1 Cor 12:13). It is a picture of the spiritual washing and regeneration by the Holy Spirit that produced a great spiritual transformation at our conversion. For example, Paul writes to Titus, "But when the goodness and loving kindness of God our Savior appeared, he saved us, not because of works done by us in righteousness, but according to his own mercy, by the washing of regeneration and renewal of the Holy Spirit, whom he poured out on us richly through Jesus Christ our Savior" (Titus 3:4–6).

Therefore, Paul reminds the Corinthians that they have a new identity in Christ and part of it means they were washed clean. They have forgiveness. Their slate was wiped clean, once and for all. As he wrote to the Colossians, "And you, who were dead in your trespasses and the uncircumcision of your flesh, God made alive together with Him, having forgiven us all our trespasses, by canceling the record of debt that stood against us with its legal demands. This he set aside, nailing it to the cross" (Col 2:13–14).

Scripture speaks to the reality of forgiveness with a number of metaphors. In the Psalms, God removes our sin "as far as the east is from the west" (Ps 103:12). In Isaiah, God completely cleanses us from the stain of sin, so that they are as "white as snow" (Isa 1:18), and He throws our sins behind his back (Isa 38:17), quite literally between His shoulder blades. In Jeremiah, God promises to remember our sin no more (Jer 31:34). The one who knows all things promises that in the New Covenant; that is, in Christ, He will treat us as if we had never sinned! In Micah 7:19, God promises to "tread our iniquities underfoot" and to cast them "into the depths of the sea." What a glorious picture of what's happened to us in Christ. Our sins are not just covered for a day, or a season, or a year. They are removed far from us and we are forgiven and washed cleaned. It is why Sam Allberry writes,

> However ingrained it may be in someone's behavior, homosexual conduct is not inescapable. It is possible for someone living a practicing gay lifestyle to be made new by God. Temptations and feelings may well linger. That Paul is warning his readers not to revert to their former way of life suggests there is still some desire to. But in Christ we are no longer who we were.[14]

Sanctified

The second reality of being in Christ is that we were sanctified when we placed our faith in the gospel. Paul is not primarily speaking of the doctrine of progressive sanctification, where we are made more and more holy. Here he is mainly talking about new identity in Christ. At conversion, we were set apart to God. We have a new identity and we are now called a "saint," or "holy one." Because of union with Christ, we are now considered a child of God and have access to God as our Father. We can approach the throne of grace with confidence and boldness (Heb 4:16). To paint a picture, we have refrigerator rights in the house of God.

This why at the beginning of 1 Corinthians, Paul greets the church as "those *sanctified* in Christ Jesus," and "called to be *saints* together with all those who in every place call upon the name of our Lord Jesus

Christ" (1 Cor 1:2). The inescapable conclusion is that if you are a Christian, you are a saint; that is, you have been given a new identity as holy before God the Father through union with Christ. To be sure, your new identity is the foundation and basis for your "progressive sanctification." Because of this, Scripture repeatedly teaches us that in order to be spiritual, we must live out who we already are (Rom 6:11–12; Gal 5:16; Eph 2:10; Phil 1:27; Col 3:1–2; Heb 12:1–2; 2 Pet 1:3–4).

This means that we are no longer ruled by or enslaved to sin (Rom 6:2, 7, 11), and therefore we have great hope when facing temptation and the enemies of sanctification. Satan is a master fisherman who baits the hook of the flesh with the lures of the world in order to ensnare and trap us, but as Christians who are loved by the Father, united to Christ, and indwelt by the Holy Spirit, we have great hope that we can mortify sin and progress in holiness (Rom 6:12–13; 2 Tim 2:21). Though sanctification will never be complete in this life (Phil 3:12–15), the Father will complete what he started in every single one of us (Phil 1:6). After all, we are His workmanship (Eph 2:10).

Justified
According to Paul, the third reality of this new identity in Christ is that we are justified; that is, we are declared righteous. Justification is a glorious truth. It is as if God is in a courtroom as judge and declares us "not guilty!" In Romans 5, Paul writes that justification occurs at

conversion (v. 1), by faith alone (v. 1) and through grace alone (v. 2). Earlier in Romans 3, Paul asserts that justification is apart from any works (Rom 3:21-31). Jesus Christ paid the debt and removed our guilt, and He provided the righteousness as a gift. Our faith is not the cause of our justification; rather, the cause of our justification is the redemptive work of Christ Jesus (Rom 3:24), and our faith is simply the means by which we are united to the righteousness of Christ, which is external to us. Like the hymn of old, we ought to sing, "Nothing in my hands I bring, simply to Thy cross I cling."

What Paul is emphasizing is that at the point of conversion, we were declared righteous and therefore presently have peace with the judge. Because we have been justified in Christ, we will be saved from the wrath of God (Rom 5:9), we have passed out of death into life (John 5:24), and there is no longer anyone who can bring a charge against us (Rom. 8:33). This understanding of free justification based on blood and imputed righteousness of Christ alone holds the only real hope that anyone has of finding acceptance with God. Praise the Lord that Paul told the Corinthians, "such were some of you, but you were. . . justified." In Christ, we are given an incredible inheritance, including adoption as God's sons and heirs (Rom 5:5; 8:15; Gal 4:5; Eph 1:5), sealing as God's possession by the Holy Spirit (Eph 1:13; 4:30; 2 Tim 1:14), and the experience of eternal life, even in the present (Rom 5:1; 14:17; John 10:10).

The Power of the Gospel Over All Sin

As we have seen, alongside our new identity, union with Christ also grants a new nature through the Spirit's work of regeneration. All of these spiritual privileges are given to us "in the name of the Lord Jesus Christ and by the Spirit of our God" (1 Cor 6:11). All three members of the Trinity are at work in this passage.

Christ is sufficient in His person and work to save and to sanctify us, working through the power of the indwelling Spirit. The Spirit empowers and transforms us through the New Covenant and renews the image of God in us. This is why Paul says in verse 11, it is "by the Spirit of our God," and later in verses 19, our body is a "temple of the Holy Spirit."

How then do we change? In 2 Corinthians 3:18, Paul says, "And we all, with unveiled face, beholding the glory of the Lord [Jesus], are being transformed into the same image from one degree of glory to another. For this comes from the Lord who is the Spirit." As we behold the sufficiency of the person and work of the Lord Jesus Christ, by the power of the Spirit we are transformed into the image of Christ. We get an "unveiled" sight of the "glory" of God the Father in the face of the Lord Jesus Christ, resulting in a transformation that is continual ("are being transformed") and ever-increasing ("from one degree of glory to another").

We must not forget the Father's role in this process. God the Father is the one who gives both the

The Gospel, the Church, and Homosexuality

Son and the Spirit, and He does so out of his eternal and infinite love. In his second letter to the Corinthians, Paul closes with this famous Trinitarian benediction: "The grace of the Lord Jesus Christ and the love of God and the fellowship of the Holy Spirit be with you all" (2 Cor 13:14). The love of God the Father began when He set His affection upon His elect in eternity past (Eph 1:3–5). Then His love was put on display when he sent His Son to die for them (John 3:16; 1 John 4:9). His love is experienced today as the indwelling Spirit pours the Father's love into our hearts (Rom 5:5), stirring up family affection for God as our Father (Rom 8:14–15; Gal 4:6–7). We cannot help but to cry out, "Abba Father!" Thus, it is only through the love of the Father that we can experience the grace of the Lord Jesus Christ and the fellowship of the Holy Spirit.

The power of the gospel, the power that enables us to live out our new identity in Christ, cannot be overstated. It must be rooted and grounded in your heart and mind so deeply that it becomes instinctive. When these truths are deep in your affections, you will instinctually know that God the Father still loves you, the Lord Jesus Christ has poured out His grace upon you, and the Spirit is fellowshipping with you and will never abandon you as an orphan, even when you are pressed by the cares and concerns of life. If you are struggling with same-sex attraction or if you know people who are, the gospel is our great hope: God the Father, who made all people in His image, has provided a way through Jesus that they can draw near to Him, and by the power of the Holy Spirit can be made new and changed.

Conclusion

When I was dating my wife, she was attending college in Southern California when the big earthquake hit in 1994. She was thrown out of her dorm bunk and had to spend the night in a field with frightening aftershocks and gas explosions going off in the neighborhood. It shook her up so bad that within a few weeks, she called me and said, "We need to take a break for a while. I need to focus on the Lord, so please don't call or write to me." I thought we were going to get married that year, but now she was saying, "I want to focus on the Lord." I remember thinking, "What am I going to do?" I was consumed with my circumstances. This woman that I love won't talk to me on the phone and won't even write to me! I handled the situation very sinfully at first. I became selfish, emotional, and depressed, wallowing in my own misery because my identity was rooted in that relationship, rather than Christ. It was one of the biggest times in my young life where God placed His hand upon me to discipline me.

But then something happened. As I began to get my eyes off myself and started serving others in my church, pouring myself into meeting their needs, my struggles and temptations with the situation, and my overwhelming desire for this relationship began to fade. Why? Paul explains in 1 Cor 6:12–20 that identity in

The Gospel, the Church, and Homosexuality

Christ is not only about us as individuals, but also about the body of Christ, the church. According to Paul, what we do with our bodies is an important issue because our body has a future (v. 13–14), our body is a member of the church (v. 15–18), and our body is not our own; we were bought with a price (v. 19–20). This means that we need community. A healthy Christian community is equipped to love and be loved and to speak the truth in love in pure ways. What's more, in community we get our eyes off ourselves and our problems, and instead on meeting the needs of others, learning by experience that what Jesus taught was true: "It is more blessed to give than to receive" (Acts 20:35).

Finally, because Christ has bought us, owns us, and has rights over us (1 Cor 6:19–20), we must glorify God in our bodies. Worship manifests itself in many ways. In the context of sexual immorality and homosexuality, the way we glorify God in our bodies is by pursuing holiness and purity. In whatever circumstances we are presently experiencing, whether we are married or single, we are called to live out who we are in Christ. We no longer have to find our identity in our sinful activities and behaviors, defined by what we have done. Instead, we glorify God for His gift of a new identity and life in Christ, embracing it by faith, and applying the gospel to our lives, keeping in step with the Holy Spirit.

3

Living Together in the Hope of the Gospel
How Shall the Church Respond to Those Struggling with Same-Sex Attraction?

Scott Denny

The Question

How the church responds to Christian men and women who struggle with same sex attraction is an important question for the church to address. It is an important question because the culture is, in fact, already answering that question for us and the world's narrative on this issue is slowly but surely creeping into the church.

The present-day narrative the world offers about same sex attraction is that people are to embrace their sexual desires for members of the same sex as being an authentic and real expression of their sexual identity. Those who do so are being applauded in our culture for being genuine about who they are. These are the brave people in our society. These are our role models. These are the ones the culture says our children are to look up to.

As this narrative grows, professing Christians are also looking to their sexual desires to define who they are; even they call this "being authentic" and "real" with who they are and with how God designed them to be. They are embracing their sexual desires as their identity and calling it good.

I submit to you that the issue of sexual identity is not the only important matter for the church to address; how we *respond* to those who struggle with homosexual desire and behavior is just as pivotal for evangelicals to address.

I say pivotal because if we respond wrongly then we jeopardize the reputation of Christ, and we harm the gospel. Let me share with you the testimony of Trey Pearson, the lead singer for the Christian band Everyday Sunday who wrote an open letter to his fans where he publicly declared that he was gay:

> I have come to accept that there is nothing that is going to change who I am.
>
> I have progressed so much in my faith over these last several years. I think I needed to be able to affirm other gay people before I could ever accept it for myself. Likewise, I couldn't expect others to accept me how I am until I could come to terms with it first.
>
> I know I have a long way to go. But if this honesty with myself about who I am, and

> who I was made by God to be, doesn't constitute as the peace that passes all understanding, then I don't know what does...
>
> It's not only an idea for me that I'm gay; It's my life. This is me being authentic and real with myself and other people. This is a part of who I am.[1]

Perhaps the most revealing thing to me about Trey Pearson was reading his admission that for more than twenty years he resisted the notion of being gay. Pearson fought against being gay and revealed in an interview that he was afraid to say anything to anyone about his feelings and desires because he feared of what the people he knew and loved would think about him.[2]

Think about that. Here is a man, a professing believer, who felt he could say nothing to anyone for fear of being unloved. I don't know this man. I don't even know if he attends a church. But I wonder how many of our brothers and sisters who struggle with same sex attraction and homosexual behavior feel they can say nothing for fear of being unloved. As a result of their silence, they no doubt wrestle with guilt, shame and perhaps even hopelessness. They may also fear saying anything to anyone, so they remain in the shadows of the church, alone and without hope.

Where this is the case, then I believe we are failing to walk in a manner that is worthy of the gospel of Jesus

Christ. Where hopelessness and despair prevail in our brothers and sisters because of this issue, then I believe we, as the church, have failed to walk worthy of our call to live together in a manner consistent with the hope of the gospel. Where shame and guilt prevail, I believe we have failed to live in a manner that is consistent with the freedom of the gospel to confess our sins and pray for one another. For the evangelical church where the gospel is the power of God for redemption and transformation, a church culture that breeds shame, guilt and silence for our brothers and sisters cannot and must not be the norm.

Let me ask you: How would you respond to a friend who confesses to you his or her struggle with same sex attraction? Should you view his or her struggle differently than any other struggle with sin? Is it even sin? Should you counsel that friend differently than another person who may struggle with lust or greed, for example?

Defining Our Terms

Before I dive in to this topic, I think it would be helpful for me to define what I mean by same sex attraction in order to avoid any confusion.

When I use the term *same-sex attraction*, I am referring to a desire for physical intimacy and affection with someone of the same sex. Same-sex attraction as I am defining it is a desire that is rooted in the heart, and it is that desire that lures and entices one toward sin (James 1:14). However, I believe that when seeking to bring hope and help to our brothers and sisters, it is important to use biblical terms. So throughout the rest of this chapter I will refer to same-sex *attraction* as same-sex *desire*.

The Power of the Gospel

The gospel's riches can never be exhausted. As we labor to bring hope and help to our brothers and sisters, I want us to hold up the gospel like a precious jewel and gaze upon it. As we do, we'll look to three of its facets—the power of the gospel, the grace of the gospel, and the truth of the gospel—as we seek to answer the question "how shall the church respond to those struggling with same sex desire?"

Paul writes in Romans 1:16-17, "For I am not ashamed of the gospel, for it is the power of God for salvation for everyone who believes, to the Jew first and also to the Greek. For in it the righteousness of God is revealed from faith for faith, as it is written, 'The righteous shall live by faith.'" The gospel reveals that there is a righteous God who demands righteousness from those who worship Him, but it is a righteousness that we cannot give Him. The gospel reveals that the righteous must live by faith. Specifically, they must live by faith in the righteousness of another, who is Jesus Christ.

As we seek to help our brothers and sisters, we first must remember that we all share the same story. We all have been changed and transformed by the power of the gospel, and this puts every one of us on equal footing. Paul writes in Ephesians 2:1-5,

> And you were dead in the trespasses and sins in which you once walked, following the course of this world, following the prince of the power of the air, the spirit that is now at work in the sons of disobedience—among whom we all once lived in the passions of our flesh, carrying out the desires of the body and the mind, and were by nature children of wrath, like the rest of mankind. But God, being rich in mercy, because of the great love with which he loved us, even when we were dead in our trespasses, made us alive together with Christ—by grace you have been saved.

Note here that we all have the same beginning—death—and we all have the same ending—glory. There is not one Christian who has done anything to merit the grace and salvation of God.

There is a scene in the movie *The Princess Bride* where the hero (who was recently killed) is brought to Miracle Max because his friends believe that Max can bring him back from the dead. In this scene, Max makes a memorable statement about our hero's condition: "It just so happens that your friend here is only *mostly* dead. There's a big difference between mostly dead and all dead. Mostly dead is slightly alive."

The Gospel, the Church, and Homosexuality

The Scriptures affirm in Ephesians 2:1 and elsewhere (e.g., Rom 3:10-18, 5:12; Ezek 37:1-6) that there is a totality to our death and to our spiritual separation from God, which leaves everyone under the same hopeless spiritual condition that we can do nothing about. We are not mostly dead. We are completely dead.

Ephesians 2:2 affirms that in our spiritual deadness, we all lived lives characterized by the pursuit of all that the world has to offer us. We all listened to the narrative of the world. We bought the lies the world offered us.

Ephesians 2:3 further affirms that we all lived lives that were characterized by the hope and belief in the things of this world, as we all sought after and pursued those things that satisfied every desire of our hearts, eyes, and minds. In the end, every single person has elevated their own desires above God Himself. This is why Paul can say in Romans 3:10-18 that there is not one person who understands, seeks after, or fears God. As such, we all by our very nature are children of the wrath of God (Eph 2:4).

Can you now see that our salvation is a miracle? Every one of us was lost. Every one of us was without hope (Eph 2:12). Every one of us was under the reign and power of sin (Rom 6:6-14). Every one of us was facing the wrath and judgment of God (John 3:36; Rom 1:18). Understanding that we all have the same beginning eliminates categories of people. We were all dead in sin—not "some of us were almost dead but we sought out God" or "some of us were worse off than others but we saw our need for God." We were all dead and without hope. Understanding that we have the same beginning compels us to look at one another with different eyes. There is none righteous, not even one.

Do you see there is no room to boast? Do you see that, but for the radical intervention of God into your life, you would be lost? Do you see that you are no more special in God's eyes than your sister who struggles with homosexual desires? Do you see that you were just as dead and without hope as she was? The gospel levels the playing field, which is what makes Ephesians 2:4 so sweet.

My two favorite words in Scripture are, "But God." But for these two grace-filled words, you would still be dead and lost in your sin. Does the way you treat others reflect that truth? These two words remind us that not only do we share the same hopeless beginning, we also share the same redeeming, hope-filled story. Consider Paul's words in Ephesians 2:4-5,

> But God, being rich in mercy, because of the great love with which he loved us, even when we were dead in our trespasses, made us alive together with Christ—by grace you have been saved—

Because of God's rich mercy, compassion, kindness, and love demonstrated toward you and me at the cross, we are no longer dead. We are alive. We are redeemed. We are forgiven. We are beloved. We are adopted. This

The Gospel, the Church, and Homosexuality

is who we are. As Christians, we are not categories of people. We are not homosexual and heterosexual. We are one people, bought with the very same precious blood of Christ.

The blood that covers the murderer covers the thief. The blood that covers the liar covers the adulterer. The blood that covers the homosexual covers the proud and arrogant and self-righteous. Because of the power of the gospel, we now share the same promise of the gospel (Eph 3:6). This is a promise of new life (Rom 6:4), a promise of new hope (1 Pet 1:3), and a promise of change and transformation (2 Cor 3:18; Rom 8:29). We all share in these promises, and so much more.

There is not a gospel for the heterosexual Christian and a gospel for the Christian who struggles with same-sex desires. There is one gospel—the power of God unto salvation for everyone who believes—and it provides the same promise for change for everyone who believes (Rom 1:16).

I want you to consider this question for a moment: Do you still struggle with some of the same sin you did when Christ saved you? I do. I still struggle with lust of the flesh, the lust of the eyes, the boastful pride of life. I still struggle with fear of man and people pleasing. My sin may manifest itself differently than yours, but it still wars in my heart. Some of you reading this chapter who may wrestle with same sex desire, know that you are no different from me. The very grace that saved you and me is the very same grace of the gospel that changes us (Titus 2:11-12).

Unlike the narrative of the world, *this* gospel narrative frees us to confess our sins and pray for one another. Without fear. Without shame. Without guilt. We are all sinners. We all need the cross. We all share the same story. We've been redeemed. Reconciled. Adopted. Washed. Cleansed.

The narrative of the world says your sexual desires define you. The narrative of the gospel says Christ's work on the cross defines you, and reminding our brothers and sisters about who they are in Christ is the greatest hope we can offer them, no matter what sin they struggle with.

If this gospel narrative fills our churches, how sweet it will be for our brothers and sisters to know that they are not alone as we confess sin together and pray together, knowing that the power and the promise of the gospel unites us into the same story.

There is no room for boasting. There are no categories. We are all in desperate need of God's grace for change.

The Grace of the Gospel

As we are changed by the power of the gospel, we must live with one another according to the grace of the gospel.

We read in Ephesians 4:1-3,

> I therefore, a prisoner for the Lord, urge you to walk in a manner worthy of the calling to which you have been called, with all humility

and gentleness, with patience, bearing with one another in love, eager to maintain the unity of the Spirit in the bond of peace.

To walk worthy is an imperative; it is a command. "To walk" is used in the Bible to mean "live," and here Paul is saying that Christians must conduct their lives together in a manner that is worthy. This word for "worthy" in the Greek literally means "to bring up the beam of the scale." Imagine, if you will, the scales of justice that need to be brought into balance. Paul is saying we must live lives that match something.

To continue in the text, Paul says that we are to "walk in a manner worthy of the calling to which you have been called." In Philippians 1:27, Paul says to walk worthy of the gospel. In Colossians 1:10, Paul writes, "walk worthy of the Lord." Here in verse one, he says to "walk worthy of the calling with which you have been called."

Truly, I think all three verses connect when speaking about the measuring stick for our lives. I think that the call he refers to here is not the call to salvation specifically (though it is not less than that), but rather I think the context implies that when God saves us, He then also calls us to be one people united around the gospel of Jesus Christ.

Unity is key for Paul in this letter. It is a unity that Paul stresses earlier in chapter two, where he reminds believers that God in Christ Jesus has made one new man in place of the two (Eph 2:15). The middle wall of separation has been removed (Eph 2:14). There is no Jew or Gentile. There is only one new man and one new people all united together in Christ (Eph 2:5). As a result, God has made us all fellow citizens and members of the same household who are joined and fit together, being built into a holy temple (Eph 2:19-21). Again, later in chapter 4, he will say that we are to grow up together in Christ (Eph 4:15).

Two inescapable things come from Ephesians 4:1-3. We are to live our lives together with other believers, and we are to live our lives together with one another in such a way that the grace of the gospel is magnified.

Our Lives Together

Paul is clear: we are to live our lives together. There is no such thing as a rogue Christian who is isolated unto herself, reading her Bible, memorizing Scripture and pursuing holiness all on her own. We cannot grow in Christ on our own. We are building blocks that are being fit together and we need each other to grow.

Secondly, in the pursuit of unity we must live grace-filled lives with one another. Paul says in verse 1 that we are to "walk worthy of our calling" and in verse 3 that we are to "make every effort to preserve our unity in a bond of peace." He says that we are to preserve unity with a certain disposition directed toward other people. These attitudes require the grace that only the gospel brings to us through God's Spirit.

These are the dispositions of humility, gentleness, patience, and loving forbearance. These are all virtues of

Christ or fruits of the Spirit (Gal 5:22-23). These are graces that God calls us to actively pursue. These are dispositions of our heart and mind and deeds that force us to depend upon Him for help. It takes the grace of God to live with people in a way that preserves unity. People are messy. People bite. Every one of these graces means that we must deny our own wants and desires. It forces us outside of our comfort zone and into the lives of others, and some of those people may make us feel uncomfortable because they aren't like us.

Let's take them one by one.

Humility

Humility engenders unity. Pride destroys. Pride puff up and exalts self.

Humility means that we enter into the lives of people we don't necessarily know or care to know. Think about that. We usually end up hanging out with people who are like us, but humility "associates with the lowly" (Rom 12:16). Pride insists on self. Humility insists on others. It takes humility to seek out others on the fringe and seek to love them and invite them into your life.

By living humbly with one another, maybe you will learn something real about each other. Maybe by living humbly with one another you learn that your brother in Christ is struggling with homosexual desires and is seeking to understand how to make sense of it all. It takes humility to admit that you're not sure how to help your brother, but you're willing to pray. It takes humility to be willing to walk over to someone you don't know in your church or small group and take time to understand their story and ask God for the grace to walk humbly with one another as you share the messiness of your lives with each other.

Gentleness
Gentleness is a fruit of the Spirit. The Greek word here is literally the idea of "power under control," or the idea of a conscious decision to exercise self-control.

Think about a lion with his mouth wide open when the trainer sticks his head inside. That lion is exhibiting power under control. He could easily snap the trainer's head clean off, but instead we admire the lion's gentleness, and we are amazed at its self-control.

What does gentleness look like in the body of Christ as we seek to preserve unity, specifically as we seek to help those facing same sex desire? It means you use self-control and restraint with the words of your mouth. It means you're careful and thoughtful about what you say and how you say it. It means you show restraint with how you speak about homosexuality. It means you don't say 'them' and 'us' when speaking about people in the church. It means you show restraint by not casually throwing around phrases like "that's so gay."

I'm not a politically correct kind of guy, but take a moment to think about it. What if your brother in Christ is struggling to fight the narrative that it's okay to be gay and be a Christian, and then he hears you say

"Oh, that's so gay" when referring to something lame you saw on Pinterest? Do you think he'll feel safe in talking to you about what's going on in his mind and in his heart?

We must be humble and gentle with how we live with one another.

Patience
Patience literally means to suffer long with people in the body of Christ. Patience makes allowance for people's shortcomings and endures with people.

Patience is truly a virtue. It is a gift of the Holy Spirit, and it is lacking greatly in me at times. Patience forces us outside of ourselves and our comfort zone, and forces us to walk alongside those who are not like us.

Patience forces us to join them in their worlds even when we feel uncomfortable being there. We need God's grace to endure with people.

To Lovingly Forbear
Forbearing in love is very similar to patience in that forbearance requires us to depend upon God for grace to tolerate those things that maybe make us uncomfortable and uneasy.

To lovingly forbear with someone who struggles with homosexuality means that you walk alongside him, not affirming his desires, but rather forbearing with him. It means persevering with him out of love because your desire is his holiness. Out a heart of love you forbear with his ups and his downs as you point him to the hope of the gospel.

Living life together under the grace of the gospel accomplishes something within the body. It creates unity. It engenders trust and fosters compassion as you take time to know one another and seek to understand someone's struggles. As you develop trust and compassion, an amazing thing happens in the body of Christ. We start by being transparent and vulnerable with one another because we feel safe with one another. This is the grace the gospel brings to us. The gospel brings us to a place of true intimacy and friendship. Too many of our friendships are built in the shallow end of the gospel. We need friendships that minister the gospel of Jesus Christ to one another in all its glorious depths. Those friendships are priceless. Those friendships require taking risks.

Do you have those kinds of friendships? If not, reach into the lives of those around you, get uncomfortable, and trust in the grace of God to meet you there, and as you do, begin to apply the truths of the gospel into the lives of others.

The Truth of the Gospel
In Ephesians 4:14-15 Paul writes,

> so that we may no longer be children, tossed to and fro by the waves and carried about by every wind of doctrine, by human cunning, by craftiness in deceitful schemes. Rather,

> speaking the truth in love, we are to grow up
> in every way into him who is the head, into
> Christ

In the life of the body, we are called to speak truth in love to one another. We've established that the gospel compels us to remember that we all share the same story, we all share the same hope and promise for change, and we all share in the call to live with one another in ways that require grace to be given to others. As we live this way, we develop a rich community that is free to love and serve one another. Part of loving one another means saying hard things to each other. It means speaking truth in love to one another because that's how we grow together.

There are two things to take away from the above exhortation.

First, notice in verse 14 that we are not to be tossed to and fro by the narrative of today that we must live according to our desires. Do not believe the narrative that says your desires define you. Do not affirm or call good what God calls evil. This kind of steadfast conviction requires a measure of maturity and growth, and such maturity and growth come from living lives together.

Secondly, Paul says that we must be prepared to speak truth in love. The literal idea here in the Greek is "truthing in love," and in order to be able to speak loving truth into the lives of people, you must know those people.

How might we get to know people? First, it's important to gain involvement in people's lives. Listen to their stories. Before you speak, it is loving to understand someone's story. Before you speak, it is loving to seek to understand why they think what they think and do what they do. It is loving to come alongside them and seek to understand them.

Application: You can't involve yourself in the lives of people you don't know. Living together implies that we show hospitality to one another and that we share community together. It means, for instance, that you regularly attend your church's worship service and worship with the people of God, and then find ways to involve yourself with those people throughout the week by attending a mid-week small group or inviting people to your home, or by going on hikes with people or hosting a BBQ. Don't wait to be invited into someone's life; go seek them out. In order to listen to someone, you must first be with them creating friendships that give you insight into their lives.

Second, give them hope and help from the gospel. Speak truth about their identity in Christ. Speak truth about the power and the promise of the gospel. Speak truth about the narrative of God's redeeming plan. Speak truth about the riches of God's mercy and speak of God's great love for them.

Application: Do you feel comfortable being able to share the riches of the gospel? Do you believe that you aren't able to help those who are struggling to make sense of their desires? Attend a counseling conference.

The Gospel, the Church, and Homosexuality

Read some good books on this issue, like *Love into Light* by Peter Hubbard or *Instruments in the Redeemer's Hand* by Paul Tripp.

Third, give accountability. If you are going to speak truth to someone, it is loving to not leave them alone. It is loving to persevere with them. It is loving to be patient with them. It is loving to sacrifice for them. It is loving to be an active participant in the ups and downs of their Christian walk.

Application: Are you in any context where you are being accountable to anyone? Are you positioning your life and the choices you make so that you are free to sacrifice your time and are able to involve yourself with your friends on deeper levels? We need each other. We can't do this without each other.

Concluding Thoughts

We are called to live our lives together in the hope of the gospel. It doesn't matter if someone struggles with the sin of homosexuality, pride, arrogance or lying. The gospel is the power of God unto salvation for everyone who believes, and we need the grace of God to live with one another in ways that exalt Christ and His gospel. We need to speak truth into each other's lives because the narrative of this world drowns out the beauty of the gospel that we so desperately need as we seek to live together in the hope of the gospel.

4

Truth with Kindness
Sharing the Gospel with the Homosexual Community

Derek Brown

In this chapter I want to help you cultivate the *character* for evangelism to those who identify as homosexual.

In one sense, we can say that nothing changes in our approach to evangelism. The gospel is the same (Rom 1:16-17). The call to repentance is the same (Mark 1:15). Christ is the same (Heb 13:8). But because the issue of homosexual identity, desire, practice, and so-called same-sex marriage is at the forefront of the cultural conversation, it is wise for Christians to discuss specifically how they might take the gospel to those who identify as homosexual.

And our *character* in how we take the gospel to those who identify this way is especially important because Scripture calls us to adorn our gospel ministry with a Spirit-wrought blend of compassion and truth-telling, love and discernment, hope and warning. We are called to model our Savior who was full of grace and truth (John 1:14).

By and large, however, the professing church appears to be tipping in either one of two directions. Either Christians are known primarily for their gospel-less condemnation of homosexuality or their uncritical acceptance of it. If we are going to be true to God's Word *and* the most useful to the homosexual community, we must intentionally pursue the kind of character that only the Spirit can produce—the kind of character Paul describes in 2 Timothy 2:22-26.

> So flee youthful passions and pursue righteousness, faith, love, and peace, along with those who call on the Lord from a pure heart. Have nothing to do with foolish, ignorant controversies; you know that they breed quarrels. And the Lord's servant must not be quarrelsome but kind to everyone, able to teach, patiently enduring evil, correcting his opponents with gentleness. God may perhaps grant them repentance leading to a knowledge of the truth, and they may come to their senses and escape from the snare of the devil, after being captured by him to do his will.

Although this passage is found in a letter designed to instruct a young pastor in how to conduct a godly and fruitful pastoral ministry, the principles Paul provides his young protégé, Timothy, are particularly relevant and applicable to us. The relevance of this passage will become even clearer as we work our way through it.

Over the next few pages, as we study 2 Timothy 2:22-26, I want us to grasp Paul's *eight essential exhortations for effective gospel ministry.*

Pursue Personal Holiness and Spiritual Maturity (vv. 22-23)

As we come to this issue of how to commend Christ to those who identify as homosexual, the first area we need to consider is *not* how to reach the homosexual community. The first area on which we need to focus is our own *personal holiness* and *spiritual maturity.* There is a logical order to Paul's instructions here. He knows it would be fruitless to admonish Timothy about how to conduct his ministry to others if Timothy was not first and foremost concerned about his own holiness. Notice the first command in our passage: "So flee youthful passions and pursue righteousness, faith, love, and peace, along with those who call on the Lord from a pure heart" (v. 22).

You are probably reading this book because you have a desire to be a useful vessel in the hands of the Lord to reach the homosexual community. You have a desire to show people the love of Christ and share the gospel with them. That's good. Scripture commends these desires. But your efforts will bear little fruit if you are walking in spiritual immaturity, sensuality, greed, and worldliness. The impure heart cannot rightly judge how to handle these kinds of volatile issues, and it will typically run from the extreme of sheer condemnation to uncritical acceptance. I believe spiritual immaturity is at the heart of the professing church's inability to approach this issue with the biblical balance of truth and love. Character, not methods, is of first importance for the Christian.

Paul first instructs Timothy and us to flee youthful passions. In other words: grow up. If you want to have an impact in a culture that is more and more departing from God's design for human sexuality, then you must first grow up. Leave behind those things that characterize those who are younger. Pursue righteousness and a deeper faith in Christ, love for God and love for others, and a life characterized by peace in your relationships (see also James 3:13-17).

If you are zealous about evangelizing people who are wrestling with homosexuality but you yourself are indulging in sexually explicit movies, unwholesome television, gossip, living in unrepentant sexual sin with your boyfriend or girlfriend, or simply pursuing a life that demonstrates very little commitment to Christ, then your attempts at evangelism will have little to no effect because people will have a hard time seeing past your hypocrisy to real Christianity.

And don't be fooled by the popular evangelical notion that you need to immerse yourself in pop-culture in order to be relevant. You will not gain a better insight into the struggles of homosexuals by watching *Modern Family*. Biblical knowledge coupled with spiritual purity will give you infinitely more insight into man's plight and the appropriate remedy than a subscription to Netflix.

David himself recognized that personal purity comes prior to speaking to others about the Lord. Consider Psalm 51:7-13:

> Purge me with hyssop, and I shall be clean; wash me, and I shall be whiter than snow. Let me hear joy and gladness; let the bones that you have broken rejoice. Hide your face from my sins, and blot out all my iniquities. Create in me a clean heart, O God, and renew a right spirit within me. Cast me not away from your presence, and take not your Holy Spirit from me. Restore to me the joy of your salvation, and uphold me with a willing spirit. *Then* I will teach transgressors your ways, and sinners will return to you (emphasis added).

It was *after* David had repented from his sin and found inward cleansing that he sought to teach others about God. But the youthful passions or lusts that Paul describes here not only include sexual purity, but also the passions of pride. This is clear from the context. Note our second exhortation.

Do Not Be Quarrelsome (vv. 23-24a)

The temptation that often ensnares immature Christians who are zealous to teach others about Christ is the temptation to be proud, arrogant, and overbearing.

When we indulge these temptations, they flow out into quarrelsome conduct. That's why Paul instructs Timothy three times to avoid quarrelling. "Having nothing to do with ignorant controversies, you know that they breed quarrels" (v. 23); "…the Lord's servant is not quarrelsome" (v. 24); "…correcting his opponents, with gentleness" (v. 25). The principle is clear: do not be quarrelsome.

Notice verses 23-24. One important way of avoiding quarreling is to "avoid foolish, ignorant controversies." In Timothy's time this referred to speculative theological arguments that did nothing for a person's edification and were usually provoked by those who were both ignorant of the issue and who had a sinful desire to start an argument for the sake of arguing.

In our day, and specifically with this issue of homosexuality, there is a temptation to delve deeply into political discussions about so-called gay marriage, legislation, and public policy. Each of these discussions have their place and should be taken up by Christians in the public square. I'm not suggesting that Christians should move out of the public discussion over these matters. Indeed, we need more courageous Christians who are willing to brave the storm of opposition to speak clearly and compassionately about these matters for the sake of our society and the temporal good of our neighbor.

But these are not the *main issues* that we should take up individually with the unbeliever in our desire to serve them with the gospel. Unbelievers cannot rightly understand how Scripture applies to public policy and legislation until the blindness of unbelief has been removed through the power of God opening their eyes to see Christ (see 2 Cor 4:1-6). There is no guarantee that a person will have a warm affinity to the truth as it relates to politics, legislation, and public policy if they are currently rejecting Jesus Christ who is the very basis for what is good and right. It's not a matter of intellectual deficiency: it's a matter of the heart's desire.

In other words, if you are attempting to bring the gospel to someone who identifies as a homosexual, it will do little good to get in a debate about the merits of our current President or the need for a conservative Supreme Court judge nominee. Are these issues about which Christians should have convictions? Absolutely, and we will see in a moment that it will be necessary for Christians to learn how to answer the most common objections to the biblical view of homosexuality. Is there a place for Christians to defend and commend biblical truths in the public arena? Yes and amen.[1] But we must plead with God for wisdom as to when and how we engage these issues with individuals. When it comes to the issue of homosexuality, we do not want to give the impression that the Christian church cares *primarily* about maintaining a moral majority or enacting certain pieces of legislation.

If your main goal is to win a debate with an unbeliever, or if you engage unbelievers with the truth of Christ mainly because you enjoy confrontation and provoking others with your verbal sparring, let me be clear: you are not ready to share Christ with the homosexual community. If your bent is to fight with others and win an argument, then you are still an immature Christian, and it is likely that your witness will do more harm than good as you engage others with the gospel.

But an effective Christian doesn't just avoid quarrels; he is kind to everyone.

Be Kind to Everyone (v. 24b)

We must be careful that the cultural conversation about this topic does not warp our minds into thinking that those who practice homosexuality are any less than human beings made in the image of God (see Gen 1:26). You might say, "Yes, but they are committing sins that the Bible denounces in no uncertain terms." Indeed they are. And so did you before Christ, and your self-righteousness that tempts you to view other sinners with contempt is even more abominable in God's eyes than sexual sin (Prov 6:17; Luke 18:9-14).

But what does it look like to be kind to everyone? One element of biblical kindness that we see from the context is that it *avoids quarreling*. So one characteristic of a Christian who is walking in kindness is that he or she will not be someone who is looking for a fight. You're not rough with others, or seeking to make them look foolish or stupid. You're not getting into spiritual conversations to display your intellectual prowess or your ability to destroy logically fallacious arguments.

The Gospel, the Church, and Homosexuality

You recognize their plight—they are without God and hope in this world, and caught, as we will see, in a trap set by our arch-enemy, Satan.

To be kind to everyone also means you recognize their humanity. They are people who have hopes and dreams and desires. They want to love others and be loved by others. They are seeking fulfillment and meaning in their lives.

To be kind to everyone means to remove unnecessary offence. It is probably unwise and unhelpful, therefore, to use words like "faggot" or to use expressions like "That's so gay" and so on.

To be kind to everyone means to be willing to listen, to get to know people, to genuinely care about their spiritual and physical well-being. "The purpose of a man's heart is like deep water, but a man of understanding will draw it out" (Prov 20:5).

As you listen, you might learn that homosexual desire is not merely about fulfilling sexual desire or mere physical attraction. Those with same-sex desire will often tell you that they are drawn to the companionship of members of the same sex more than they are of the opposite sex.[2] You might learn that those who have same-sex sexual desire cannot truly remember a time when they "chose" to have such desires.

Be Able to Teach (v. 24c)

But Paul does not call us merely to cultivate in us a spirit of kindness. For kindness to be *Christ-like* kindness, it must be melded to biblical conviction. What am I talking about here? Think of Christian kindness like a giant redwood. The redwood provides shade from the heat for weary travelers; it provides a home for various animals and insects; it's fragrant and beautiful and attractive. It will not reach out to hurt you. It is a servant to you and to the animals of the forest. But try as you might, you cannot budge it. You can push and pull and yell and scream but you cannot move a giant redwood tree. That is Christian kindness. When it comes to the content of the gospel and the call to repentance, servants of Christ must be kind and gentle with others, yet immovable and unshakable in their convictions.

No matter what the world or even some professing evangelicals say about homosexuality, the true Christian will always remain undaunted and unmoved in his or her conviction that homosexual practice is a sin from which we must repent if we would be saved from eternal damnation. "Do not be deceived," Paul says in 1 Corinthians 6:9-11. If you continue in your practice of same-sex sexual immorality, you *will not* receive the kingdom of God. The same goes for you reading this book who may not be struggling with homosexuality but who are living in unrepentant sexual sin with your girlfriend or boyfriend. You will not enter the kingdom of God.

But God has given Christ to sinners out of His love and grace, and He calls to *all* men and women to come to Christ right now for forgiveness and cleansing. Remember, in the same passage that Paul warns those who continue in sexual sin that they will not enter the kingdom of God, he also indicates that there were some within the Church who had been saved and cleansed from a similar lifestyle: "such were some of you" (1 Cor 6:11).

You don't need to look inside of yourself for any qualifications for whether or not you have a warrant to come to Christ. You don't need to perform any good works before you come to Christ. You don't need to clean up your life before you come to Christ. You come to Christ first and receive His mercy and grace and forgiveness and cleansing, *then* you begin a life of holiness and purity. You come to Christ *for* holiness, but you don't come to Christ *by way of your* holiness. There are no conditions that you must meet before you come to him. Listen:

> **Jesus:** "Come to me all who labor and are heavy laden, and I will give you rest" (Matt 11:28).
>
> **Paul:** "Believe in the Lord Jesus Christ and you will be saved" (Acts 16:31).

A person's business right now if they are outside of Christ is to believe in Christ for salvation, regardless of who they are or what they have done.

You must be able to assure those who are currently unbelieving that Christ offers them full forgiveness of sin and the power to change, and He is able to offer this because he died on the cross to pay the penalty for all the sins of those who believe in Him. Jesus Christ lived a perfect life in the place of sinners and died on the cross in place of sinners, thus fully satisfying God's justice so that God remains just while declaring an ungodly person righteous when they believe in Jesus (Rom 3:26).

If we are going to have any impact at all, we must be able to teach these vital truths of the gospel of Christ.

But there are other areas in which Christians must have competence if they are going to have an impact on the homosexual community. I will mention two important areas.

> (1) *Progressive Sanctification* – The fight for holiness is a life-long fight, and not all sexual temptation is eradicated at conversion. Habits that were entrenched before conversion will often need much work to root out of the life. Growth in holiness is usually slow and plodding. Spiritual growth is often described in agricultural terms because it takes time.

> (2) *A Biblical Vision of Human Sexuality* – We will examine this topic in some detail in the next chapter. But suffice it to say right now that Christians who are going to have an impact in this area of evangelism will need to have some sturdy knowledge of God's design for human sexuality.

The Gospel, the Church, and Homosexuality

If we are going to have an impact with the gospel in the lives of unbelievers, we must have clarity on some important biblical truths and refuse to back down from those truths. Not because we are obstinate, but because we love Christ and because we know that *only* the truth can truly help anyone. Compromising the truth may get us some favor in the short term, but it will only serve to harm people eternally.

Answering Objections

But there is a danger in narrowing in on only a few areas, for a Christian cannot only be courageous in the area of homosexuality. We must be courageous in everything the Bible teaches. To be able to teach means that you will need to learn how to answer some of the major objections to the biblical view of homosexuality.

For an excellent and accessible resource to help answer some of the most common objections to the Bible's teaching on sexuality, I recommend without qualification Kevin DeYoung's *What Does the Bible Really Teach About Homosexuality*.[3] I will briefly answer a few of the most common objections.

What About "Gay Marriage?"

Although this isn't the main issue with which you have to deal with the unbeliever, you should be able to present an accurate biblical portrait of human sexuality and show, from that portrait, why marriage is a moral/ontological/metaphysical reality established by God that cannot be redefined by man or by the state (see Genesis 2:21-25). In the biblical sense, marriage between members of the same sex cannot exist, and there are many reasons why we should not accept gay marriage as a wholesome and good alternative to traditional marriage.[4] Furthermore, Christians cannot accept gay marriage because such acceptance is not only accepting something that is not true; it also condones an institution in which the sin of homosexual practice is committed.

What About Love?
Shouldn't love between two people be the determining factor in whether or not they should be considered "married" or engage in sexual activity? With this objection you will need to offer a clear reason why our human conception of what love entails cannot be a reliable guide to what is morally acceptable. Why? Because our desires are fallen, easily corrupted, and can often be set upon the wrong object. If our personal "loves" are the only factor in determining the goodness of a relationship, there is no logical reason to oppose outright immoral relationships like pedophilia or polygamy. Clearly, a standard other than our subjective feelings must determine what kinds of relationships are right and wrong.

Isn't the Bible Merely Prohibiting Promiscuous Same-Sex Relationships?
Another common objection, often posed by those who have some knowledge of the Bible, is that Scripture only

prohibits promiscuous same-sex sexual activity. In other words, it is morally acceptable if one engages in same-sex activity, so long as it is within a committed and faithful relationship. Sam Allberry explains this objection.

> One of the arguments commonly made today in favor of same-sex partnership is that what must surely count above all else in faithfulness and commitment. Shouldn't faithfulness within a relationship be what determines its moral goodness rather than the gender of those involved in it? A promiscuous gay lifestyle with multiple partners and one-night stands might be wrong, but two people who love each other and are faithful to whatever promises they have made—surely that's OK?[5]

But will Scripture allow for this category of faithful and committed homosexual activity? Allberry answers this objection by referencing Paul's response to a situation at the church in Corinth. A man and woman were involved in a sexually immoral relationship, but the apostle maintains his stance that they must be removed from membership in light of their unrepentant sin. Allberry continues,

> Paul does not ask about their level of commitment or whether they are being faithful. That is not the issue. Whether or not

> they are in a long-term committed relationship is beside the point; the fact remains that it is wrong and should be not be happening. Paul does not distinguish between faithful illicit relationships and profligate illicit relationships, as if the latter are out of bounds but the former might just squeak in by virtue of their faithfulness. Consistency and faithfulness while sinning in no way diminish the sin.[6]

Again, like what we said about "love" in the section above, one's level of commitment or faithfulness to their partner does not determine the morality of a particular sexual act or activity. Biblically, homosexual sexual activity is sinful, whether or not it occurs within a committed relationship.[7]

Doesn't the Bible Also Endorse Slavery?
It is sometimes argued that to oppose gay-marriage and homosexual sexual union on the basis of the Bible's prohibition is to be inconsistent because the Bible endorses slavery. If you are going to be consistent by prohibiting homosexuality, the argument goes, then you must also promote slavery. Again, however, this argument fails to recognize that marriage, unlike slavery, is rooted in *creation*.

DeYoung explains,

> Unlike slavery, the church has always been convinced that (until very recently) that

homosexual behavior is sinful. There are not biblical passages that suggest the contrary. There are, however, passages in Scripture that encourage the freeing of slaves (Philem 15-16) and condemn capturing another human being and selling him into slavery (Ex. 21:16; 1 Tim 1:8-10). To make it sound like the Word of God is plainly for slavery in the same way it is plainly against homosexual practice is biblically indefensible.[8]

What About Other Sins Like Divorce and Gluttony?
Sometime this objection is used to point out Christian hypocrisy, or inconsistency, or to lessen the seriousness of the issue. It is true: Christians should shun hypocrisy and seek to be as consistent as possible in their own lives. Christians should not be guilty of pointing out certain sins at the exclusion of others. Christians should take all sin seriously. And to the degree that some Christians and churches are not taking serious these sins (divorce and gluttony), to that degree should they be admonished. But it is important to remember that gluttony is not mentioned in any of Paul's "vice-lists." Kevin DeYoung observes,

> Some will be surprised to learn that *gluttony* appears in none of the New Testament vice-lists. In fact, most of the Bible is overwhelmingly positive about food. . . . If the New Testament has an overriding

> concern with food, it is that God's people not be overly concerned about it. . . . No honest reader of the NT can deny that Jesus and the apostles were much more concerned about what we do sexually with our bodies than with the food we eat.[9]

With regard to divorce, although a serious matter in God's eyes, the biblical prohibitions against it allow for some exceptions (Matt 5:32; 19:9; 1 Cor 7:10-16); the prohibition against homosexuality, however, does not.

God Doesn't Want Me to Be Miserable and Unfulfilled

You're right. God does not want you to be miserable and unfulfilled. He sent Christ so that you might be eternally happy and satisfied in God. Yet, there are some who claim that they experienced greater happiness and fulfillment, even in their relationship with God, once they stopped fighting and yielded to their sexual desires. DeYoung explains,

> But, as the stories go, once they learned to embrace their God-given identity and reconcile their faith with their sexual orientation, many "gay Christians" have discovered a new vibrancy in their walk with God. If embracing their sexuality were really a step away from God, revisionist authors ask, why are so many "gay Christians"

spiritually flourishing? A healthy tree cannot bear bad fruit, and a diseased tree does not bear good fruit (Matt 7:18).[10]

Is this a legitimate objection? While DeYoung wants us to make sure we are not unfeeling or indifferent toward those who express that they are miserable in their walk with Christ, he also wants us to understand that the "good fruit" to which the Scripture speaks is not necessarily feelings of fulfillment.

> The "good fruit" Jesus talks about in Matthew 7:15-20 is not a reference to my sense of satisfaction or my perceived ministry effectiveness. The next verses make it clear that laboring in Jesus name, even with impressive results, is no guarantee of entering the kingdom of heaven (vv. 21-23). Bearing fruit means doing the will of our Father who is in heaven (v. 21). Jesus is looking for followers who will hear his words and put them into practice (vv. 24-27). No matter how we feel about ourselves or what others think about our effectiveness in the church, there are no genuinely healthy trees apart from obedience to Christ and the fruit of the Spirit (Gal 5:16-24).[11]

There are some who have same-sex sexual desire who come to Christ who find the joy and peace of forgiveness and a clean conscience, who still wrestle with same-sex sexual temptation for the rest of their lives. There are also many testimonies of those with homosexual desires who have come to Christ and found great change and renewal of their desires. But in the case of *every* Christian, we all know that eternal happiness will mean some temporal suffering and self-denial in this life (Acts 14:22; Rom 8:17; 2 Cor 4:17). Jesus says, "Blessed [happy] are those who mourn, for they shall be comforted" (Matt 5:4). Therefore, it is unwise to use our perceived sense of fulfillment as a gauge of whether or not we are walking in faithfulness to Christ.

Christians Are Hate-Filled Bigots
To be sure, there are professing Christians who are hate-filled bigots, but they aren't true Christians (1 John 4:7-8). A Christian who maintains that homosexual practice is a sin of which a person must repent if they are going to inherit eternal salvation, who opposes same-sex marriage because it is the place in which same-sex sexual practice occurs, and who graciously offers the gospel to sinners, cannot be called a bigot in any meaningful sense of the word.

The Gospel, the Church, and Homosexuality

Christians Just Want to Restrict the Happiness of those who have Same-Sex Attraction

The Christian's motivation for holding the line on the issue of homosexual practice should be: (1) love and reverence for God and His Word (Matt 22:37); and (2) love for one's neighbor (Matt 22:39). Christians don't want to restrict the happiness of those who have same-sex attraction; on the contrary: they want to increase it for all eternity! Joy can only come through repentance and faith in Christ. To remain in unrepentant sin will end in eternal misery (Rev 20:13). If one is led to believe they can continue in their sin of homosexual practice and still inherit the kingdom of God, then whomever has told them this lie is guilty of profound hatred, not compassion.

Patiently Endure Evil (v. 24e)

But a Christian must not only be able to teach others and have some ability to answer a few common objections to what the Bible teaches on the topic of homosexuality, it is also vital that we know how to patiently endure evil. It is no wonder why Paul includes this piece of instruction in this section. No matter how kind or merciful you are to those entrenched in unbelief, if you, like that big Redwood, hold firmly to the truth of the gospel, there will be some—perhaps many—who will oppose you and start bringing out the chainsaws and the hatchets. So, you must patiently endure the evil of persecution and misrepresentation and slander.

But there's more to this instruction than an

encouragement to graciously bear personal attack. A Christian who has a renewed mind and heart is now able to behold the reality of God and His Word in the world. And if you are paying attention to what is going on in our society, you will be weighed down by how much evil is rampant in our society. The evil that surrounds the Christian can become a burden and trouble the soul. This is always how God's people have responded to societal evil. The Psalmist wept when he surveyed the cultural landscape and saw a wasteland of unbelief. Psalm 119:136: "My eyes shed streams of tears because people do not keep your law."

But there may be some here today who find themselves rather unbothered by the state of our nation. You are emotionally undaunted and unmoved by the massive moral shift that has occurred over the last three years. You blithely say, "Ah yes, we all know mankind is evil. Plus, this is the way the Bible said it's going to go." But be careful that you are not mistaking emotional apathy for spiritual maturity. The Psalmist wept.

The mature, growing Christian will be someone whose heart may be often weighed down by the sinfulness of the society around him; that is why Paul tells us to patiently endure evil. What evil? The evil committed against us, and the evil committed against God in the greater society. Patience is vital because the temptation will be to lash out at those who are the most outspoken in their rebellion.

Correct Your Opponents with Gentleness (v.25a)

Paul's exhortation here harkens back to his instruction to "be able to teach." We must be able to "correct" those who are not walking in the truth. The assumption is that there is such a thing as truth and error, and that we are called to correct those who are currently believing what is wrong. We must have the courage to say, "That is incorrect," or "Scripture does not teach that," or "Here is what the Bible really says."

But there is a specific way Scripture calls us to speak the truth to others. Paul says, "with gentleness." He is simply following the rich instruction of the Old Testament. Consider a few selections from the Proverbs:

> **Proverbs 15:1:** "A soft answer turns away wrath, but a harsh word stirs up anger."
>
> **Proverbs 15:4:** "A gentle tongue is a tree of life…"
>
> **Proverbs 25:15:** "With patience a ruler may be persuaded, and a soft tongue will break a bone."

Gentleness also implies patience and tenderness, as though one is caring for a plant or a new child. The seed of the word takes time to grow, and it needs to be cultivated carefully and gently. This is how Christ deals with us. Listen to Isaiah's prophetic description of the Messiah.

> Behold my servant, whom I uphold, my chosen, in whom my soul delights; I have put my Spirit upon him; he will bring forth justice to the nations. He will not cry aloud or lift up his voice, or make it heard in the street; a bruised reed he will not break, and a faintly burning wick he will not quench; he will faithfully bring forth justice (Isa 42:1-3).

These exhortations are not referring to soft-spokenness, as if talking in hushed tones is especially Christ-like. Gentleness has to do with knowing when and how to press the truth on someone and when to back off. It has to do with being patient for the other person to learn and grasp the truth and for the Holy Spirit to water the seed that you've planted. It means you're not easily offended or outraged.

It also means that you recognize—because you know your own heart—that it is difficult to hear the truth and to be corrected. It levels our pride. It is devastating and heart-rending at times to finally admit that what we've believed for most of our life is wrong. When you are correcting your opponents—those who disagree with a biblical view of sexuality—you must do it with gentleness or else your words will be largely ineffective. To be fierce and hard and combative only causes a person to harden their heart and redouble their defenses. But, as Proverbs 25:15 says, "a soft word will break a bone." A gentle and humble conduct among those who oppose biblical Christianity actually serves to soften them and prepare them for the truth.

Remain Rooted in the Sovereignty of God (vv. 25b)

But all of these instructions to exercise kindness and gentleness and patience and steadfastness are not calls to muster up our will power. Everything that Paul has just said is grounded in understanding and believing a profound theological reality: *God* is the one who grants repentance and saves people from the snare of the devil. This truth together with the next truth in verse 26 combines to devastate our pride and frustration toward unbelievers.

If you're a Christian today, you are not a Christian because you penetrated the divine mysteries with your intellect, or because you are better than others. It is *only* because God granted you repentance, out of grace and mercy alone, and pulled you out of a pit of sin and selfishness. On what basis can you look down on those who are walking in unbelief? You would be right there with them if it weren't for the grace of God.

And it wasn't that God gave you some grace and you figured out the rest, as though you were caught in a pit and God threw a rope down to you and you climbed out. No, the Bible teaches that you were in a pit all right, but you were dead in that pit (Eph 2:1-3). God had to bring you back to life, draw you out of the pit, and place you on secure footing by Himself. When this truth settles deep into your heart and mind, you will be inclined to treat your opponents with gentleness and kindness. And we are able to keep teaching the truth in all its fullness because we know it is God who grants repentance that leads to the knowledge of the truth.

In our contemporary culture, the temptation will be to remove the sharp edges of what Scripture says about sexuality in order to make the message more relevant. But this is an unnecessary concession. The text tells us that knowledge of the truth comes *from* repentance. That is, a person cannot fully embrace and approve of what Scripture says about sexuality until they are willing to repent of their rebellion against God and submit to His Word. And it is only God who can grant this repentance. Therefore, diluting what the Scripture says about homosexuality will not help anyone or ultimately prove useful. It only makes the message more palatable to the unredeemed mind. Knowing, however, that it is God who must open the eyes and grant repentance enables us to teach the truth in all its fullness, for we know that God will grant repentance leading to a knowledge of this truth.

Recognize The Real Enemy (v. 26)

Finally, the danger of writing books on homosexuality and mounting large-scale theological responses to these important cultural issues is that we can give the impression that homosexuals are the enemy. Well, we have an enemy, and it isn't homosexuals or the LGBT community; it is the Serpent of old who deceives the whole world (Rev 12:6). Our text makes this clear. The reason why we pursue holiness and spiritual maturity, conduct ourselves with kindness and gentleness, and hold fast to biblical truth is because we believe God is sovereign over salvation *and* because those with whom we share the gospel are ensnared by the enemy of all mankind. As Paul tells us in his second letter to the Corinthians, unbelievers are blinded by the enemy so that they are unable to see the "light of the gospel of the glory of Christ" (2 Cor 4:4). Our hope is that God grants people repentance so that "they may come to their senses and escape from the snare of the devil, after being captured by him to do his will" (v. 26).

In light of this truth our first move toward those who are rejoicing and reveling in their sin is not disdain or disgust, but broken-hearted compassion and kindness. Such people have been captured by our enemy and are ignorant of spiritual realities. In one sense, they know what they are doing (Rom 1:32), but in another sense, they don't know what they are doing (see Eph 4:18). They may not understand it fully, but they are enslaved by their sin and blinded and controlled by Satan (Eph 2:1-3). And if you are a Christian today, you were in the exact same place prior to God rescuing you and granting you repentance. How can we, therefore, feel any self-righteousness or disdain or disgust toward those who are captured and enslaved but unaware of their dire situation? What do we have that we did not receive by God's free grace (see 1 Cor 4:7)?

When we grasp these twin truths of God's sovereignty and the dire spiritual situation in which our friends and neighbors and colleagues find themselves, we will be enabled to walk in gentleness *and* steadfast commitment to the truth. As God's grace and Holy Spirit forms this kind of character in us, I believe we will find fruitfulness in our efforts to take the gospel to the LGBT community.

5

Something Good, and Something Even Better: A Biblical Vision of Human Sexuality

Derek Brown

Over these past few chapters we've discussed specifically the issue of homosexuality and how the church might respond in grace and truth to those who identify themselves as gay or homosexual. As we come to the closing chapters of this book, however, we want to leave you with a full-orbed biblical vision of human sexuality. We want to end this way for three inter-related reasons.

To Equip You
We want to equip you with a glorious vision of God's design and plan for human sexuality so that you might serve as salt and light in a culture that does not understand the meaning of sex and has utterly disregarded the biblical vision as prudish, unnecessarily restrictive, and generally unfulfilling. If you are going to persuade others of the goodness of God's design for

human sexuality you must first see it for yourself in Scripture.

To Guard You

We also want to guard you from two potential pitfalls. First, we want to guard you from mere negative responses to the issue of homosexuality. You will have nothing to offer those who identify themselves as gay or homosexual if you can *only* say that homosexuality is sin. By painting a clear, contoured picture of God's design for marriage and human sexuality, you will be able to, by way of contrast, help others to see how unnatural and unfitting homosexuality is and how good and wise God's design is.

Second, a biblical vision of human sexuality will keep you from turning sexuality into an idol. When it comes to sex, many if not most folks in our society seem to think that a person cannot be truly fulfilled or happy without sexual intimacy. A biblical vision of human sexuality, however, shows us that sex, though a good—even wonderful—gift from God is not ultimate, but actually points to a greater spiritual reality. A biblical vision of human sexuality also teaches us to value singleness and equips us with the knowledge that one does not need to be married or engage in sex in order to find true fulfillment and joy.

To Sustain You

Finally, we want to leave you with a robust vision of human sexuality in order to uphold you as you wade through the unbelief and sensuality of our culture. You may be tempted at times to wonder if homosexuality is really something that undermines God's design for human sexuality and over which Christians should trouble themselves. You may be tempted to forsake sexual purity with your boyfriend or girlfriend because you don't see the point of preserving your purity until marriage. Whatever the case, a clear vision of God's design for human sexuality will help sustain your faith and obedience as you face the unremitting opposition of our larger society.

Back to the Beginning:
Man and Woman Made in God's Image

So where do we begin in our aim to craft a biblical vision of human sexuality? We start in the beginning, with the origin of marriage in Genesis 2.

In Genesis 1:26-31, we see that God formed man and woman in His own image and placed them on earth to exercise dominion over it and God's manifold creatures. The man and woman were to work and subdue and rule over this world as God's vice-regents. That men and women were meant to exercise rule over the world is implied in the word "image" and the language of dominion.

Genesis 1:26-31 gives us a broad description of what occurred on day six, while Genesis 2:1-25 fills in the details.[1] In Genesis 2:7 we learn that God formed the man out of the dust of the ground and breathed into his nostrils the breath of life, making him a living creature. God then plants a garden and places the man in it to work it and keep it (Gen 2:15). This is language of labor ("work") and protection ("keep"). After instructing the man about how to conduct himself in the garden—explaining to the man that all the abundance of the garden belonged to him, except the tree of the knowledge of good and evil (2:16)—God notes, for the first time, that something is "not good" in the garden.

This is an important discourse marker because all through Genesis 1:1-31 God is found repeatedly stating that His creation is good. The phrase, "And God saw that it was good," is a refrain throughout the first chapter of Genesis (Gen 1:10, 12, 18, 21, 25). Now something is not good. What is the problem? Man is alone.

Now, let's ponder over these words for a moment. The man was there *with God*. How could this not be a good situation? It was not good because God never intended man to exist by himself without human companionship, even if the man was alone with God.

So God brings to the man all the animals He had previously created in order for Adam to name them, but also to show him that his life companion would not be found among these creatures.

> Now out of the ground the LORD God had formed every beast of the field and every bird of the heavens and brought them to the man to see what he would call them. And

whatever the man called every living creature, that was its name. The man gave names to all livestock and to the birds of the heavens and to every beast of the field. *But for Adam there was not found a helper fit for him* (Gen 2:19-20, emphasis added).

There was not found a helper *fit for him*. These animals were good, but they wouldn't work as Adam's helper. Why not? Because they were not made in the image of God. Only an image-bearer would be suitable to be the man's helper. How does God remedy this situation?

> So the LORD God caused a deep sleep to fall upon the man, and while he slept took one of his ribs and closed up its place with flesh. And the rib [or side] that the LORD God had taken from the man he made into a woman and brought her to the man (Gen 2:21-22).

God is going to take *from* the man in order to make a helper *for* the man.

> And the rib that the LORD God had taken from the man he made into a woman and brought her to the man. Then the man said,
>
> This at last is bone of my bone, and flesh of my flesh, she shall be called Woman, because she was taken out of Man (Gen 2:23).

The way the woman is formed and the way Adam responds to her shows us what it means that she is "fit" for him. She is bone of his bones and flesh of his flesh. She is the same—she is made in the image of God—but she is different: she is a woman and *not* a man. That's why Adam says that she will be called woman (*ishah*) because she was taken out of man (*ish*). Both sameness and difference are highlighted in this passage. She is a suitable fit because she is a human being, but also, and just as important, because she is a woman she is different from the man in significant ways. She looks different: her physical features, body, and anatomy are different from the man's physical features, body, and anatomy. But the differences are not merely physical; she is *entirely* female, while he is *entirely* male.

Same, Yet Different

The complementary nature of the man and woman's design is seen in the fact that the woman was taken *from* the man. It is important to note that the narrative tells us that Adam was created from the dust of the earth. Eve, however, is not created in the same way that the man was created; she created from Adam's rib. She is fully human, but clearly different than the man. She was taken from the man to then be joined back together with the man, and they can only be rejoined because they are sexual counterparts. They *fit* together physically. And they not only fit together physically, but emotionally, intellectually, and spiritually as well. In

The Gospel, the Church, and Homosexuality

God's wisdom, He has so created man and woman that we complement each other in a myriad of ways.

At this point in the narrative, Moses reflects on his current situation—he wrote this passage in 1400 B.C., so marriage had been around for a long time already—and he explains why a man leaves his father and his mother and why he joins his wife in sexual union. This pattern is not the result of an arbitrary tradition that somehow developed over time or through the alleged process of evolution. A man will leave his father and his mother and join to his wife because God created man and woman to come together in marriage as a one-flesh union. This one flesh union is a spiritual *and* physical union. That Moses has in mind sexual union in this text is clear in the following verse: "And the man and his wife were both naked and were not ashamed" (Gen 2:25).

Here, in a concise yet elegant prose, and a little bit of poetry, God describes the origin of and His intention for human sexuality. Human sexuality is a glorious, intensely pleasurable, and fruitful gift. It is designed to weld a husband and a wife together in a physical and spiritual and emotional union that cannot be broken or compromised without severe disruption and pain. It is designed to bring forth children as the fruit of the love that a man and a woman have for each other. The very bodies of husbands and wives were designed to be joined together in sexual union, with intricately designed nerve structures for immense pleasure and reproductive capacities for the bearing of children.

The Entrance of Sin and the Perversion of Sexual Intimacy

Human sexuality is a good gift from a good—joyful—Creator. But something happened. Adam and Eve were tempted by our arch enemy, Satan, that great serpent of old, to disobey God and thus introduce sin into this world and into our experience. Now our hearts are infected with the tendency to *pervert* God's good gifts, and this infection has spread to every aspect of our personhood.

How we think and feel about God, about each other, how we treat each other, and how we think and feel about sex has been infected with sin. We now perceive God and the world and each other and sex with clouded vision and corrupted desires. We now want the wrong things in the wrong way, or we want the right things in the wrong way or at the wrong time. Our hearts no longer desire God's good gifts the way He intended them to be desired.

For example, you may be a married man, but your heart desires a woman other than your wife. Those desires, as Jesus tells us, are a kind of adultery with the heart (Matt 5:28-30). To act on those desires is actual adultery—not an affair or a fling, but adultery (Ex 20:14). You may be an unmarried woman, but you may be yielding to your sexual desires and sleeping with your boyfriend. You may be a single woman who is only attracted to other women and you have acted on those desires. You may be a single man who is indulging in pornography and masturbation. None of these desires or actions fulfill God's intended use for His good gift of human sexuality. These desires and actions are perversions of what is good, and they are a result of the infection of sin that affects every single person reading this book.

Hearts and Minds Recreated Through Christ

But even though sin has infected the world and infected our hearts, the sexual relationship between a husband and wife is celebrated throughout the entire Bible, and with great joy and exuberance. The Song of Solomon and Proverbs 5:15-23 are unashamed celebrations of sexual pleasure between a husband and a wife. In the New Testament, Paul tells us that sexual intimacy is a gift that God intends married couples to enjoy often (see 1 Cor 7:2-6).

Through the gospel, the forgiveness of sins, and the renewal of the Holy Spirit, God has recreated our hearts to enjoy and think about sex the way He has always intended it to be enjoyed and thought about for our good and for His glory. You may have a sexual past riddled by your own sin or by the sin of others against you. Jesus Christ is in the business of restoring and healing your heart and mind so that you might once again think and feel about sex the right way.

The Unfittingness of Homosexual Practice

With regard to the topic of this book, we must note that it is because of man and woman's complementary design and the beauty of God's design of the sexual relationship between a husband and a wife that homosexual practice is forbidden by Scripture. In every sense of the word, homosexual practice is *unfitting*. The bodies of same-sex couples do not possess the complementarity of the man and the woman together. Reproduction is impossible in same-sex intimacy, and often the body can be damaged through same-sex sexual activity. Why? Because our bodies were not made for same-sex intercourse.[2]

God's Word tells us that homosexual desire and homosexual practice are not natural; they are the unnatural fruits of humanity's fall into sin and the corruption of our hearts.

Marriage is Glorious, but Not Ultimate

But even though sexual intimacy between a husband and a wife is a glorious gift, it is not ultimate. The pull and tug of sexual desire, though incredibly powerful, is not meant to point to itself, but to something even greater. And this is *good news* for everyone in this room—whether you are married or single, or whether you struggle with homosexual desire or not. Why did God create marriage and sexual intimacy between a husband and a wife? To be a living parable of Christ's relationship to His church. This is not mere poetic-sounding rhetoric. God designed marriage between a man and a woman—including the sexual intimacy—to put on public display an earthly picture of what it looks like for Christ to love and care for His bride, the church. Let's examine this truth briefly in Ephesians 5:22-33.

Wives, submit to your own husbands, as to the Lord. For the husband is the head of the wife even as Christ is the head of the church, his body, and is himself its Savior. Now as the church submits to Christ, so also wives should submit in everything to their husbands. Husbands, love your wives, as Christ loved the church and gave himself up for her, that he might sanctify her, having cleansed her by the washing of water with the word, so that he might present the church to himself in splendor, without spot or wrinkle or any such thing, that she might be holy and without blemish. In the same way husbands should love their wives as their own bodies. He who loves his wife loves himself. For no one ever hated his own flesh, but nourishes and cherishes it, just as Christ does the church, because we are members of his body. "Therefore a man shall leave his father and mother and hold fast to his wife, and the two shall become one flesh." This mystery is profound, and I am saying that it refers to Christ and the church. However, let each one of you love his wife as himself, and let the wife see that she respects her husband.

Due to space constraints we are unable to examine this text in its fullness (although we will look at it in a little more detail below). Nevertheless, what I want you to notice is that Paul, under the inspiration of the Holy Spirit, reveals to us a mystery; namely, that marriage is meant to be a picture of Christ's relationship with his bride. Christ loves His bride and lays down his life for her, so the man is to do the same. The church submits to and follows Christ's loving and humble leadership, and the woman is to follow her husband in the same way. Christ nourishes and cherishes His bride, so the man is to do the same.

Then, pointing back to Genesis 2:24, "Therefore, a man shall leave his father and mother and hold fast to his wife, and the two shall become one flesh," Paul concludes, "This mystery is profound." Now, it is important to understand what the word "mystery" means in the New Testament. It does not refer to something that is difficult to discern or something strange or suspenseful. A mystery is simply something that was not revealed in the Old Testament that is now revealed in the New Testament. Paul says, "This mystery is profound, and I am saying that it refers to Christ and the church." In Genesis 2:22-25, where we have a beautiful description of God's creation of marriage between a man and a woman, Paul says this institution pointed to something even greater: Christ and his church. Someday, Christ's bride will be married to him forever:

> Then I heard what seemed to be the voice of a great multitude, like the roar of many waters and like the sound of mighty peals of

thunder, crying out, "Hallelujah! For the Lord our God the Almighty reigns. Let us rejoice and exult and give him the glory, for the marriage of the Lamb has come, and his Bride has made herself ready; it was granted her to clothe herself with fine linen, bright and pure"—for the fine linen is the righteous deeds of the saints. And the angel said to me, "Write this: Blessed are those who are invited to the marriage supper of the Lamb." And he said to me, "These are the true words of God." (Rev 19:6-9)

Even before the earliest days of creation, God planned that marriage between a man and a woman would serve as a living parable of Christ's relationship to His church—a husband and his bride (Gen 2:24; cf. Eph 5:22-32). Although the parable will one day fade away, the reality to which it points will live forever. Thus, the male and female counterparts of earthly marriage are essential to its very definition, and they will be until Christ returns and receives his bride, the corporate church.

And this is good news for everyone reading this book. But how?

For Married Christians

If you are married, God has called you to be a living picture of Christ and his church. Husbands, you are to lead and love and lay down your life like Jesus Christ did for his bride. Wives, you are to follow your husband's leadership with joy and respect, as the church does to Christ. This is massive privilege and stewardship.

And God calls you to glorify Him in a *particular way* through marriage. This means that whether or not you glorify God in your marriage hinges on each of you fulfilling the roles and responsibilities that God has laid out in His Word. God is wise, and He is good, and He has designed marriage in such a way that he receives the most glory and you receive the most joy and satisfaction *when and only when* we are living according to these specific roles and responsibilities. And God provides these roles and responsibilities throughout the Scripture, but most explicitly in Ephesians 5:22-33.

Paul begins by addressing wives: "Wives, submit to your own husbands, as to the Lord" (Eph 5:22). The first instruction is for a wife to submit to her husband. What does this mean? The word submission when applied to women is controversial in our day. Most of the time it is controversial because it is not rightly understood. God's instruction to the wife here is not a call to become her husband's slave or servant, nor is it a call to thoughtlessly do whatever the husband says. It is simply a call to gladly follow her husband's leadership.

In his good design, God has made the man to be the leader of the home. The man is the one who sets the vision for the family and makes sure that Christ remains at the center of the home. He also bears the burden of making difficult decisions that affect the family. The wife is to gladly respond to this leadership. Why? The next two verses tell us: "For the husband is the head of the wife, even as Christ is the head of the church, his body, and is himself its Savior. Now as the church submits to Christ, so also wives should submit in everything to their husbands" (Eph 5:23-24).

A woman's submission to her husband is not arbitrary: it is a reflection of the church's submission to Jesus. And how does the church submit to Jesus? By gladly following and trusting His leadership. But here's an important point that married couples need to remember. The husband is *not* Jesus. Every Christian husband, though justified in Christ, is still a sinner, and his leadership will never be perfect. In fact, if a husband ever attempts to lead his wife into sin, the woman's submission to Jesus overrules her submission to her husband. This is what it means to love Jesus supremely (see Matt 10:37-39; Luke 14:26-27).

But there is also another problem. Not only is the husband a sinner, but the wife is also a sinner. As we learn in the Genesis narrative, when Adam and Eve disobeyed God's command to not eat the fruit of the tree of the knowledge of good and evil, they fell into sin and ruin and became sinners by nature (Gen 3:6ff).

At the core of their being they now had a tendency to disobey God and go against His design. We are told in Genesis 3:16 that this means that for the woman, her tendency in the marriage will be to rule over your husband—to usurp his authority and to take his place. When this happens, neither the husband nor the wife will be happy or satisfied for long. But by God's grace, a woman can grow into a wife who not only follows her husband's leadership, but affirms and encourages it.

But this means that husbands must be the kind of men that their wives will be happy to follow. And that is why Paul gives twice as much space in this passage to exhort the husbands. Scripture says,

> Husbands, love your wives as Christ loved the church and gave himself up for her, that he might sanctify her, having cleansed her by the washing of water with the word, so that he might present her without spot or wrinkle or any such thing, that she might be holy and without blemish" (Eph 5:25-27).

Husbands are called to love their wives like Christ loved his church. And how did Christ love his church? He laid down his life for her. He died for her. He gave everything for her eternal good. Husbands, this means that you must die. You must die daily. You must die to selfishness, to fear, to laziness, to getting your own way. You must win your wife's confidence and trust by always speaking the truth, by protecting her purity, by making good decisions—and good second decisions when the first one is foolish.

It means that men must also die to—and this is very important—to passivity. Just as we saw in Genesis 3:16 that the wife's temptation will be to usurp the husband's leadership role, so it will be the man's temptation to become passive and to neglect to lead. So husbands must die to the temptation to live in their marriages passively.[3] This means you must actively seek to set the tone for your family, to provide for your family, to instruct your children in the fear and admonition of the Lord (Eph 6:4), and to actively pursue your wife's sanctification (Eph 5:25-26). You must guard her from her spiritual enemies and go to battle for her soul as you seek to wash her in the pure water of the Word of God.

When Adam and Eve sinned, God came to Adam first (see Gen 3:9). It may have been Eve who ate the fruit first, but it was Adam who was held responsible for the welfare of the family. This means that if there are problems in the family—even problems caused by the woman—God holds the husband responsible to seek solutions to the problem and pursue reconciliation when there is a fight or an argument. The man's unique responsibility to lead in this way doesn't mean the woman is exempt from seeking reconciliation; it means that God holds husbands responsible to initiate reconciliation—even if it was the woman's fault.

Paul also instructs the husband to nourish and cherish his wife as if she was his own body. How do we care for our own body? We feed it, we provide for it, we clean it, we protect it. Why? Because she is your own body. "Therefore a man shall leave his father and mother and hold fast to his wife, and the two shall become one flesh" (Eph 5:31).

In God's design, he intends for a husband and wife to live together in spiritual, emotional, and sexual unity.

The wife's joy is now the husband's joy, and the husband's joy is now the wife's joy. The wife's pain is now the husband's pain, and the husband's pain is now the wife's pain. This also means that the marriage relationship now has priority over every other relationship and why Genesis 2:24 tells the couple that they must leave their closest relationships and cleave to one another.

If you are married, God has called you to glorify Him by fulfilling your specific roles and responsibilities in marriage. This is a high calling. Marriage is not ultimate, but while we are on earth, our marriages are meant to reflect the love and leadership of Christ and the happy submission of His church.

For Single Christians

What if you're single? "If marriage and sexual intimacy are so glorious," you might wonder, "how can this be good news for me?" It is good news because human marriage and sexual intimacy are only temporary. They are—get this—*shadows* of an infinitely greater spiritual reality. Earthly marriage and sexual intimacy will someday give way to the reality to which they point. God is going to renew and remake this earth and these heavens (Rev 21:1). God is going to restore our bodies at the resurrection (John 5:29; Phil 3:10-11, 21). In the future, God is going to dwell with his people in intimate fellowship for all eternity, and we will live and work and play and serve Him with new bodies on a new earth. But there will be one major difference, however. There will be no human marriage. Jesus told the Sadducees that at the resurrection there will be no more marrying and giving in marriage (Matt 22:29-33). Why? Because earthly marriage will give way to the reality to which it always pointed: Christ's marriage to His bride.

In a real sense, therefore, if you never fulfill your desires for marriage and sexual intimacy, you haven't really lost out on anything. You have merely bypassed the shadow on the way to the reality. You bypassed the preview for the movie; the postcard of Yosemite National Park for an actual trip up Half Dome.

Even the natural family—husband, wife, and children—is not ultimate. The Christian single man or woman belongs to a spiritual family that is greater than the natural family, as Jesus often explained in the Gospels (Matt 12:48-49; Mark 3:33-35; 10:29-30). Jesus acknowledges the goodness of the natural family: he exalts marriage (Matt 19:1-12) and upholds the command to honor one's father and mother (Matt 15:1-9). Nevertheless, he places one's spiritual relationship to himself and His people above the earthly family (Matt 10:34-39; Mark 10:29-30).

Indeed, we learn in the Gospels that one of the reasons Jesus came (!) was to divide earthly families (Matt 10:34-35). When someone trusts in Jesus and is born again, their loyalties fundamentally change. Loyalty to Jesus is now supreme and more important than loyalty to earthly parents and family. This is not to denigrate the natural family, but only to demonstrate that the family of God takes ultimate priority even over the natural family. The point is this: *God's family is eternal; the natural family is temporary.*

We must also keep in mind that, like marriage, singleness is also a gift (1 Cor 7:1-40). In 1 Corinthians 7:1-40, Paul seems to assume that marriage is the normal state (7:1-5). The apostle does not command singleness, but he commends it (7:6-7, 26-27) and recognizes that singleness is a gift that not all possess (7:7-9). But Paul also acknowledges that singleness has serious advantages (7:28; 32-35). Singleness is a time to pursue to "undistracted devotion to the Lord" (v. 35) not to exult in unfettered freedom from responsibility in order to indulge in feeding one's own desires and interests. As John Piper puts it, "And with this promise [of blessings in the age to come that are better than the blessings of marriage], there comes a unique calling and a unique responsibility. It is not a calling to extend irresponsible adolescence into your thirties."[4]

Nevertheless, with this warning of misusing one's singleness notwithstanding, singleness has significant advantages when it comes to serving the Lord. For example, when I graduated college I was unmarried. I lived in southern California with the family of one of my good friends from college. I substitute taught in an elementary school and served at my friend's church for about two months until another college friend introduced me to a full time job as a youth pastor in the San Francisco Bay Area. I didn't have to think about whether my wife would want to move or consider how changing jobs and locations might affect my children. I prayed. I decided. And then I packed up all of my belongings into my Jeep Grand Cherokee and drove the six hours north to Sunnyvale. There was a freedom in singleness to serve the Lord that I no longer have. I love my wife and my three kids with all my heart, but I am now unable to take the kinds of risks I used to or spend the kind of time I would sometimes like to spend working on ministry related projects or discipleship or preaching.

Furthermore, as Piper notes, the single life uniquely displays vital truths about Christianity.

- "The truth that the family of God grows not by propagation through sexual intercourse, but by regeneration through faith in Christ;"
- "The truth that relationships in Christ are more permanent, and more precious, than relationships in families (and, of course, it is wonderful when relationships in families *are* also relationships in Christ; but we know that this is often not the case);"
- "The truth that marriage is temporary and finally gives way to the relationship to which it was pointing all along: Christ and the church—the way a picture is no longer needed when you see face-to-face;"
- "The truth that faithfulness to Christ defines the value of life; all other relationships get their final significance from

this. No family relationship is ultimate; relationship to Christ is."⁵

Therefore, the single man or woman can produce and raise a spiritual offspring (Isa 53:10; 56:4-5; 1 Cor 4:15; Col 3:10). Now, God's renewed image is perpetuated by conversion (see Col 3:10).

That is why Paul could say that he was the spiritual father to many (see 1 Cor 4:15). Single men and women play a vital part in discipling young children. Although there is some loss and unfulfilled desire, these afflictions are momentary and are actually producing an eternal weight of glory (2 Cor 4:17-18).

For Those With Homosexual Desires

If you are a Christian and you wrestle with homosexual desires, Christ can change you and your desires. For some, this change happens immediately. For others, it may take a long, long time. Others may find that their desires never fully leave them.

As we've seen in the very nature of God's design of human sexuality, marriage with a member of the same sex is an ontological impossibility, and sexual intimacy with a member of the same sex is forbidden by God's Word because it is a direct violation of His wise plan and good commandments. So the celibate single life may be the only option for you. You may feel alone in this struggle. Let me assure you that you are not. The Church is God's gift to you. It is in the Church that you can find fellowship, comfort, and helpful admonishment to persevere in your faith, despite your sexual struggles (see Heb 3:12-15). And there are many Christians who have fought this battle and have remained celibate for the glory of God despite their sexual desires.[6]

Given the nature of the struggle for those who have same-sex desire, here are some questions for married folks. Are you actively looking to enfold single people into your lives? Are you making it appear that you are superior to single people merely because you are married? Do you imply, by the way you talk about marriage and singleness, that the single life is a second-tier option for the Christian? If we are going to have an impact for Christ's sake with those in the homosexual community, we must make singleness with Christ an attractive alternative. Jesus dignified singleness and demonstrated conclusively that a person *does not* need to me married to fulfill his or her Christian calling. As we saw earlier in this chapter, singleness holds many advantages for Christian ministry. The single Christian life is a worthy calling.

But even here we must be careful to uphold Jesus' words. He tells us that if we don't take up our cross and follow Him, we are not worthy of Him (Matt 10:38). If we are going to be Jesus' disciple, we must be willing to live with unfulfilled desires as Christ sees fit. We must be willing to die—to pick up our cross—not just ultimately in martyrdom, but to specific desires, like marriage.

How can we do this? Because Jesus is holding out the promise of unimaginable joy in the new heavens and the new earth that is coming soon for all Christians. You can set aside some desires now because you know that God will someday see to it that you only and ever experience true spiritual, holy satisfaction and fulfillment in his presence forever (Ps 16:11). For those who don't want to hold out in faith for that wonderful promise, choosing instead to continue to indulge in sexual activity that is clearly against God's Word, God's eternal punishment awaits for rejecting His good promise. There is much at stake.

Conclusion

Human sexuality is a gift. Marriage is a gift. Both are precious and must be treated with utmost care and respect. God promises terrible things for those who disregard the holiness and beauty of marriage and sexuality. The sexually immoral, the adulterers, and those who practice homosexuality, will not inherit the kingdom of God unless they repent and turn from their sin and turn to Christ (see 1 Cor 6:9-11; Heb 13:4).

But even though marriage and sexuality are good and glorious gifts, they are temporary gifts that will someday give way to an even better reality. Because of this truth, let us press on with hope that our struggles and trials now will someday fade into memory when we stand before the Lord Jesus, clothed in his righteousness, cleansed from all our sin, and in our right minds, once and for all.

6

Conclusion
Changing Nation, Unchanging Mission

Derek Brown

Changing Nation, Unchanging Reality
President Obama was certainly right when he said, in his congratulatory phone call to James Obergefell on Friday, June 26, 2015 that Obergefell's leadership had "changed the nation."[1] Yes, an entire nation will be different–fundamentally–due to this landmark decision by the Supreme Court of the United States. Marriage, previously recognized as an institution that can only, by definition, exist between a man and a woman, is now declared by an act of judicial will to exist between members of the same sex.

But the church knows that such a brazen misreading of our nation's founding documents doesn't really change anything. Yes, the requirement of states to legally recognize gay "marriages" is now the law of the land, but laws of lands, though externally binding upon the citizens of a given nation, have no power whatsoever to change moral realities created and sustained by God. Jesus Christ is the same yesterday, today, and forever (Heb 13:8), and His Word will always remain (Matt 24:35).

Even before the earliest days of creation, God planned that marriage between a man and a woman would serve as a living parable of Christ's relationship to His—a husband and His bride (Gen 2:24; cf. Eph 5:22-32). Although the parable will one day fade away, the reality to which it points will live forever. Thus, the male and female counterparts of earthly marriage are essential to its very definition, and they will be until Christ returns and receives His bride, the corporate church. It is arrogance in the extreme to suggest that a nation can overthrow with a 28-page decision[2] what God designed and founded from the beginning of time and plans to fulfill at the end of it.

Changing Nation, Unchanging Mission

Like marriage, the church's mission also remains the same. The danger of mounting large-scale theological responses to the folly of such legal decisions is that they might give the impression that homosexuals are the enemy; that those who are fighting for what they believe is a fundamental right of human personhood should be simply opposed, silenced, and condemned.

The theological responses must be made, to be sure, for even the friendliest evangelicals who uphold a biblical vision of marriage and have the courage to point out governmental inconsistency and lawlessness will be castigated by popular media and classified as bigots. But the notion that the homosexual community poses a threat to the church or that our ministry to them should consist merely of condemnatory refutations is far from the Spirit of Christ.

What cannot be lost in the fray is the clear conviction that Jesus saves sinners, and those who are rejoicing at this earth-shaking decision and everything it stands for are precisely those Jesus came to save. Christians who know personally the ravages of sin and who have tasted of God's forgiveness in Christ cannot stand idly by while the homosexual community marches unchecked into behaviors and lifestyles that will destroy them, nor can we give the impression by what we say and how we talk that their sin places them beyond the reach of God's grace. Christ tells the silent church: speak the truth courageously and in love. He tells the self-righteous church: such were some of you.

Changing Nation, Unchanging Truth

For Christians, some things never change. Christ doesn't change, marriage doesn't change, our mission doesn't change, and the gospel doesn't change. The church's response to our government's formalized defiance of God's design for and definition of marriage, then, will draw from a few key truths.

1. The Bible is the Word of God. That we have in our possession the revealed and inerrant word of God is a truth relevant in any season. A nation's laws may drift from the intention of her founding fathers, religious opinion may sway with the winds of popularity and social comfort, cultural norms will ebb and flow, but God's Word never changes (Isa 40:7-8). Our understanding of marriage and appropriate sexual expression between people made in God's image must always be drawn from divine revelation. The temptation to yield to popular opinion or to mistake doctrinal compromise for "love" and "grace" is great, and many professing Christians have already swallowed the bait of pseudo-kindness by simply choosing the path of least resistance. But the true church will always remain tethered to the Bible, for it is her life, her light, and the source of her stability.

2. The Gospel is a Call to Repentance. No matter what trends in our greater culture, the gospel will always be a call to turn from sin and trust in Christ. That means the greedy person must turn from their greed, the thief from his stealing, and the homosexual from their practice of homosexuality. Of course, our call for genuine repentance must not imply that all once-practicing homosexuals will find all their same-sex desires eradicated at the moment of their new-birth; struggles will likely remain, and heterosexual desires may never fully replace homosexual ones.[3] But we must firmly maintain that the goodness of the gospel is found not only in the freedom of forgiving grace, but in the power of transforming grace, and that Christ readily provides the ability to obey His commands to those who come to Him looking for justification *from* their sin, not justification of it.

3. Compassion Requires Truth-Telling. If the Bible is true when it says that those who persist in sin will not go to heaven but will instead face eternal punishment from a holy God, then genuine compassion will never hide the truth, but proclaim it without compromise. The apostle Paul knew that such truths would never be popular and that professing Christians and false teachers alike would look for ways to blunt the sharper contours of the gospel. That's why he often warns the church to avoid deception, especially when the majority is saying that unrepentant sin is no big deal.

> Or do you not know that the unrighteous will not inherit the kingdom of God? *Do not be deceived*: neither the sexually immoral, nor idolaters, nor adulterers, nor men who practice homosexuality, nor thieves, nor the greedy, nor drunkards, nor revilers, nor swindlers will inherit the kingdom of God (1 Cor. 6:9-10, emphasis added).

Paul's point, of course, is not to say that such sinners cannot come to Christ for salvation (many have and still do today); rather, the apostle is warning that those who continue in these sins without true repentance–regardless of their profession of religion–will not go to heaven (see also Gal 5:19-21; Eph 5:3-6). It is actually an expression of profound *hatred* to lead a practicing homosexual (or adulterer or fornicator) to believe that he or she can continue in their sexual practice and boast in a right standing with God. What could be more hateful than perpetuating a lie? What could be more compassionate than telling them the truth?

4. The Church Best Upholds Marriage Through Complementarianism. It may not be readily apparent right now, but the intramural debate among Christians concerning male and female roles and responsibilities in the home and in the gathered community of believers relates directly to this recent SCOTUS decision. I believe that the stance evangelical churches will take with regard to so-called gay marriage will be determined, in large measure, by where they are now or plan to be in the near future with regard to the issues of complementarianism and egalitarianism.

How can I make such a claim? Because at its core the debate over complementarianism and egalitarianism is about the differences between men and women. To the degree that the church diminishes these good differences through egalitarianism and evangelical feminism, to that degree does it weaken the ground by which she can build a case against gay "marriage." Some feminists already see this connection and are calling for greater consistency. It seems that at some point the logic of egalitarianism must concede to the logic of so-called gay marriage, for both seek to diminish the differences between genders. Egalitarian churches may not support so-called same-sex marriage today, but it appears inevitable for the future.

5. The Church Serves the LGBT Community By Offering a Biblical Alternative To Marriage. In their honest and insightful article at *The Gospel Coalition*, Rosaria Butterfield and Christopher Yuan argue that the church has failed to provide the LGBT community with a compelling vision of singleness where those who now follow Jesus in the obedience of celibacy (instead of homosexual practice) can find love and fulfilling ministry as a member of God's family.

> We have failed to show the LGBT community another option to marriage—which is singleness—lived out in the fruitful and full context of God's community, the family of God. This does not mean, as Justice Kennedy wrote, that singles are "condemned to live in loneliness," but that singles can have intimate and fulfilling relationships full of love. This is not a consolation prize. It can be just as rewarding and fulfilling as marriage.

> Defining marriage as being between a husband and a wife appears unfair to the LGBT community, in part because a life of singleness is seen to be crushingly lonely. Have we in the church inadvertently played into that lie with our idolatry of marriage while being pejorative and silent toward singleness? If singleness is unfair, then it's no wonder marriage has become a right. Just as the LGBT community appealed to the rest of the world for dignity and respect, it's time for the church to fight for the dignity and respect of single women and single men.[4]

We will do much good for the LGBT community when we recapture the biblical vision for singleness, where those who are unmarried, far from living in a second-class Christian existence, are able to carry out their calling before God faithfully and fruitfully (see 1 Corinthians 7:1-40). The church's ministry to single adults is vital in our response to the legalization of gay "marriage."

What Man Means for Evil God Means for Good

At basic, the church's response to the recent Supreme Court decision is the same for this season as it would be for any season. Christians must hold fast to the Scripture and to the gospel, ready to weather the storms of marginalization and misrepresentation, eager to love sinners and call them to repentance. Some things will never change.

But it is our hope that as the church is battered by a culture that is increasingly hostile to Christ and His Word, we may become sweeter to people as we become even more steadfast in truth; gentler with sinners as we become even stronger against sin. Who knows? Our reflection on this SCOTUS decision many years from now may bring us to conclude that, like the cross of our Lord Jesus, what man meant for evil, God meant for good—eternal, sin-forgiving, God-glorifying, people-saving, church-building, Christ-exalting, heaven-opening, Satan-defeating, good. I pray it so.

Notes

Chapter 1—Introduction

1. Albert Mohler, *We Cannot Be Silent: Speaking Truth to a Culture Redefining Sex, Marriage, and the Very Meaning of Right and Wrong* (Thomas Nelson, 2015), 11.
2. See our list of helpful books in the appendix.
3. For example, take Matthew Vines in his book *God and the Gay Christian* (Convergent Books, 2015). You can read a thorough response to this book edited by Al Mohler *God and the Gay Christian? A Response to Matthew Vines* (SBTS Press, 2014).
4. Westboro Baptist Church, for example, can often be found in public places using such hateful speech without any reservation.
5. Preston Sprinkle, *People to be Loved: Why Homosexuality is not just an Issue.* (Grand Rapids: Zondervan, 2015) 20.
6. Ortlund, Ray. "How to build a gospel culture in your church." *TGC National Conference*, 2015.
7. Ray Ortland *The Gospel: How the Church Portrays the Beauty of Christ.* (Crossway: Wheaton, 2014), 72.
8. Yuan, Christopher. *A Christian Response to Homosexuality.* Round 1: Workshop for the 2015 TGC National Conference.http://resources.thegospelcoalition.org/library/a-christian-response-to-homosexuality.

Notes

Chapter 2—The Gospel and Homosexuality

1. Peter Hubbard, *Love into Light: The Gospel, the Homosexual and the Church* (Greenville, SC: Ambassador International, 2013), 19-23.
2. Hubbard, *Love into Light*, 23.
3. Hubbard, *Love into Light*, 24.
4. Hubbard, *Love into Light*, 26.
5. Hubbard, *Love into Light*, 27.
6. All English translations of Scripture are from the ESV unless otherwise noted.
7. Brad Hambrick, *Do Ask, Do Tell, Let's Talk: Why and How Christians Should Have Gay Friends* (Minneapolis, MN: Cruciform Press, 2016), 18.
8. Kevin DeYoung, *What Doe the bible Really Teach About Homosexuality* (Wheaton, IL: Crossway, 2015), 145.
9. Sam Allberry, *Is God Anti-Gay? And Other Questions About Homosexuality, the Bible, and Same-Sex Attraction* (Purcellville, CA: The Good Book Company), 8-9.
10. Allberry, *Is God Anti-Gay*, 30.
11. Rosaria Champagne Butterfield, *Openness Unhindered: Further Thoughts of an Unlikely Convert on Sexual Identity and Union with Christ* (Pittsburg, PA: Crown & Covenant Publications, 2015), 106.
12. DeYoung, *What Does the Bible Really Teach About Homosexuality*, 65.
13. Allberry, *Is God Anti-Gay*, 35-36.
14. Allberry, *Is God Anti-Gay*, 37.

Chapter 3—Living Together in the Hope of the Gospel

1. Gil Kaufman, "Christian Rock Star Trey Pearson Comes Out to Fans in Emotional Letter," *Billboard.com*,

June 2, 2016, http://www.billboard.com/articles/news/7393337/christian-rock-star-trey-pearson-comes-out-to-fans-in-emotional-letter. Accessed April 26, 2017.

2. Annie Martin, "Christian Singer Trey Pearson Comes Out as Gay," *UPI*, June 2, 2016. Accessed April 26, 2017, http://www.upi.com/Entertainment_News/Mus-ic/2016/06/02/Christian-singer-Trey-Pearson-comes-out-as-gay/3681464883767/. Accessed April 26, 2017.

Chapter 4—Truth with Kindness

1. An excellent resource for helping you thinking biblically through the various political and social issue presently facing American Christians is Wayne Grudem, Politics According to the Bible: A Comprehensive Resource for Understanding Modern Political Issues in Light of Scripture (Grand Rapids: Zondervan, 2010).

2. Along with my experience in personally counseling those who struggle with same-sex attraction, Wesley Hill's book *Washed and Waiting: Reflections on Christain Faithfulness and Homosexuality* (Grand Rapids: Zondervan, 2010), helped me understand that homosexual desire is not always purely sexual. The desire for physical intimacy coincides with a preference for same-sex companionship over opposite-sex companionship. This is an important insight, and will aid us in counseling those with same-sex attraction. Although I think Hill relies too heavily on Catholic authors in his book and uses the unhelpful phrase, "Gay Christian" to describe those who believe in Christ but struggle with same-sex attraction, I recommend this book to help you better think though the internal and

social struggles that a Christian in this situation must bear. For more on the problems with the phrase "Gay Christian," see my review of Hill's book, *Spiritual Friendship: Finding Love in the Church as a Celibate Gay Christian* (Grand Rapids: Bazos, 2015) in *The Journal of Biblical Manhood and Womanhood* 20.2 (Fall 2015) and Owen Strachen "Should the Church Speak of 'Gay Christian'" in *The Journal of Biblical Manhood and Womanhood* 19.1 (Spring 2014), 4-7

3. Kevin DeYoung, *What Does the Bible Really Teach About Homosexuality* (Wheaton, IL: Crossway, 2015).
4. See Daniel Heimbach's *Why Not Same-Sex Marriage: A Manual for Defending Marriage Against Radical Deconstruction* (Sisters, OR: Trusted Books), 2014.
5. Sam Allberry, *Is God Anti-Gay? And Other Questions About Homosexuality, the Bible, and Same-Sex Attraction* (Purcellville, VA: The Good Book Company, 2014), 39.
6. Allberry, *Is God Anti-Gay*, 39-40.
7. See also Robert Gagnon, *The Bible and Homosexual Practice: Texts and Hermeneutics* (Nashville: Abingdon Press, 2001), 340-361 for a detailed answer to the objection that the Bible only condemns exploitive, pederastic forms of homosexuality.
8. DeYoung, *Homosexuality*, 107.
9. DeYoung, *Homosexuality*, 92.
10. DeYoung, *Homosexuality*, 117.
11. DeYoung, *Homosexuality*, 117-18.

Chapter 5—Something Good, and Something Even Better

1. I take the first and second chapters of Genesis as complementary descriptions of one creation account, not two different creation stories. It has been argued by some biblical scholars that the author of Genesis

presents us with distinct creation stories that cannot be reconciled with respect to the chronology of the man and woman's creation, and should, therefore, be read symbolically. The text of Genesis, however, does not require that we propose two different creation accounts. Instead, a better and more natural solution is to see Moses providing us in Genesis 1:26-31 with a broad description of man's creation on day six, to then turn in Genesis 2:1ff to give a detailed description of what occurred on that day. In Genesis 1:26-31, we are told that God created both the man and the woman on the sixth day. Genesis 2:1ff tells us that Adam and Eve came into existence in a particular order: the man first, then the woman. See Derek Kidner, *Genesis: Introduction and Commentary* (Downers Grove, IL: Intervarsity, 1967), 58; C. John Collins, *Genesis 1-4: A Linguistic, Literary, and Theological Commentary* (Philipsburg, NJ: P & R, 2006), 108-112.

2. For an eye-opening discussion of the harmful effects of same-sex sexual intimacy, see Robert Reilly, *Making Gay Okay: How Rationalizing Homosexual Behavior is Changing Everything* (San Francisco: Ignatius, 2014). See also my review of Reilly's book at *The Gospel Coalition*, https://www.thegospelcoalition.org/article/making-gay-okay.

3. For an extended discussion of the problems that arise from male passivity, please see Derek Brown, *Strong and Courageous: The Character and Calling of Mature Manhood* (Sunnyvale, CA: GBF Press, 2017), particularly chapter one: "One Man's Passivity: Twelve Observations on Male Leadership from Genesis 2-3."

4. John Piper, *This Momentary Marriage: A Parable of Permanence* (Wheaton: Crossway, 2009), 113.

5. List taken directly from Piper, *This Momentary Marriage*, 106.

Notes

6. See Sam Allberry, *Is God Anti-Gay?: And Other Questions About Homosexuality, the Bible and Same-Sex Attraction* (Purcellville, VA: The Good Book Company, 2013). Alberry has also developed a website called LivingOut.org to help Christians who wrestle with same-sex attraction pursue holiness, celibacy, and sexual purity.

Chapter 6—Conclusion

1. Emma Roller, "Watch President Obama Call Jim Obergefell to Congratulate Him on the Gay-Marriage Ruling," *The Atlantic*, June 26, 2015. https://www.theatlantic.com/politics/archive/2015/06/watch-president-obama-call-jim-obergefell-to-congratulate-him-on-the-gay-marriage-ruling/455073/. Accessed, March 23, 2017.
2. You can find the full text of the Supreme Court's majority opinion at https://www.supremecourt.gov/opinions/14pdf/14-556_3204.pdf.
3. See Peter Hubbard, *Love into Light: The Gospel, the Homosexual, and the Church* (Greenville, SC: Ambassador, 2013).
4. Rosaria Butterfield and Christopher Yuen, "Something Greater than Marriage," The Gospel Coalition, June 30, 2015. https://www.thegospelcoalition.org/article/something-greater-than-marriage. Accessed July 1, 2015.

SCRIPTURE INDEX

Genesis
1:10   100
1:12   100
1:18   100
1:21   100
1:25   100
1:26   76
1:1-31   100
1:26-31   99
2:1-25   99
2:7   99
2:15   100
2:16   100
2:19-20   101
2:21-25   82
2:22-25   108
2:23   101
2:24   101, 108, 109,
            114, 122
2:25   103
3:9   113
19:5-11   34

Exodus
20:14   104
21:16   85

Leviticus
18:22   34, 35

Leviticus
20:13   35

Psalms
16:11   120
51:7-13   73
103:12   40
119:136   90

Proverbs
5:15-23   105
6:17   76
15:1   91
15:4   91
18:24   26
20:5   77
25:15   91, 92

Isaiah
1:18   40
38:17   40
40:7-8   124
42:1-3   92
53:10   118

Jeremiah
31:33-34   25
31:34   40

Ezekiel
37:1-6	55

Micah
7:19	40

Matthew
5:4	88
5:28-30	104
5:32	86
7:15-20	87
7:18	87
7:21	88
7:21-23	88
7:24-27	88
10:34-35	115
10:34-39	115
10:37-39	111
10:38	119
11:28	79
12:48-49	115
15:1-9	115
19:1-12	115
22:29-33	114
22:37	88
22:39	22, 89
24:35	122

Mark
1:15	69
3:33-35	115
10:29-30	115

Luke
14:26-27	111

Luke
18:9-14	15, 76
19:10	21

John
1:14	69
3:16	45
3:36	55
5:24	43
5:29	114
10:10	43
15:15	26

Acts
14:22	88
16:31	79
20:35	47

Romans
1:16	10, 16, 57
1:16-17	53, 69
1:18	55
3:10-18	55
3:21-31	42
3:23	24
3:24	43
3:26	43
3:26	80
3:27-31	42, 43
5:1	42, 43
5:2	42
5:3-5	35
5:5	43, 45
5:9	43
6:2	42

Romans

6:4	57
6:6-14	55
6:7	42
6:11	42
6:11-12	42
6:12-13	42
8:9	29, 30
8:14-15	45
8:15	43
8:17	88
8:29	57
8:33	43
12:5	16
12:16	61

1 Corinthians

1:2	41
4:7	17
4:15	118
5	36
5:4-5	36
5:13	36
6:9	29, 36, 31, 33
6:11	38, 39, 44, 79
6:12-20	46
6:13-14	46
6:15-18	47
6:18	32
6:19	44
6:19-20	32, 47
7:1-5	116
7:1-40	116, 128
7:2-6	105
7:6-7	116

1 Corinthians

7:7-9	116
7:10-16	86
7:26-27	116
7:28	116
7:32-35	116
7:35	116
12:13	40

2 Corinthians

3:18	44, 57
4:1-6	75
4:17	88
5:17	25
13:14	45

Galatians

4:5	43
4:6-7	45
5:16	42
5:16-24	87
5:19-21	125
5:22-23	61
6:7-8	35

Ephesians

1:3-5	45
1:13	43
2:1	55
2:1-3	93
2:1-5	54
2:2	55
2:3	24, 55
2:4	55, 56
2:4-5	56

Scripture Index – 140

Ephesians	
2:5	60
2:10	42
2:12	55
2:14	60
2:15	59
2:19-21	60
3:6	57
4:1-3	58-59, 60
4:14	65
4:14-15	64-65
4:15	60
4:18	95
4:30	43
5:3-6	125
5:5	33
5:22	110
5:22-32	109, 122
5:22-33	106-07, 109
5:23-24	111
5:25-26	113
5:25-27	112
5:31	113
6:4	113

Philippians	
1:6	25, 42
1:27	42, 59
3:10-11	114
3:12-15	42
3:21	114

Colossians	
1:10	59
2:13-14	40

Colossians	
3:1-2	42
3:5	30
3:10	25, 118

1 Timothy	
1:8-10	85
1:10	29, 36

2 Timothy	
1:14	43
2:21	42
2:22	71
2:22-23	71
2:22-26	70, 71
2:23	74
2:23-24	73, 74
2:24	74, 76, 77, 89
2:25	74, 90, 92
2:26	94, 95

Titus	
2:11-12	57
3:4-6	39

Philemon	
15-16	85

Hebrews	
3:12-15	118
4:15	30
4:16	41
12:1-2	42
13:4	120
13:8	69, 122

Scripture Index — 141

James
1:13-15	26, 30
1:14	52
1:19	13
3:13-17	72

1 Peter
1:3	25, 57

2 Peter
1:3-4	42

1 John
4:7-8	88
4:9	45

Revelation
12:6	94
19:6-9	109
20:13	89
21:1	115

RECOMMENDED RESOURCES

Sam Allberry, *Is God Anti-Gay? And Other Questions About Homosexuality, the Bible, and Same-Sex Attraction.* Purcellville, VA: The Good Book Company, 2014.

Rosaria Champagne Butterfield, *The Secret Thoughts of an Unlikely Convert: An English Professor's Journey into Christian Faith,* Expanded Edition. Pittsburg, PA: Crown and Covenant, 2014.

Rosaria Champagne Butterfield, *Openness Unhindered: Further Thoughts of an Unlikely Convert on Sexual Identity and Union with Christ* (Pittsburgh, PA: Crown & Covenant Publications, 2015), 106.

Kevin DeYoung, *What Does the Bible Really Teach About Homosexuality.* Wheaton, IL: Crossway, 2015.

Robert Gagnon, *The Bible and Homosexual Practice: Texts and Hermeneutics.* Nashville: Abingdon Press, 2001.

Brad Hambrick, *Do Ask, Do Tell, Let's Talk: Why and How Christians Should Have Gay Friends.* Minneapolis, MN: Cruciform Press, 2016.

Daniel Heimbach's *Why Not Same-Sex Marriage: A Manual for Defending Marriage Against Radical Deconstructio*. Sisters, OR: Trusted Books.

Peter Hubbard, *Love into Light: The Gospel, the Homosexual and the Church*. Greenville, SC: Ambassador International, 2013.

R. Albert Mohler, ed., *God and the Gay Christian? A Response to Matthew Vines*. SBTS Press, 2014.

R. Albert Mohler, *We Cannot Be Silent: Speaking Truth to a Culture Redefining Sex, Marriage, and the Very Meaning of Right and Wrong*. Nashville: Thomas Nelson, 2015.

Preston Sprinkle, *People to be Loved: Why Homosexuality is not Just an Issue*. Grand Rapids: Zondervan, 2015.

ABOUT THE AUTHORS

MICHAEL SANELLI is minister of youth and music at Grace Bible Church in Pleasant Hill, California and adjunct professor at the Cornerstone Bible College and Seminary in Vallejo, California.

DEREK BROWN is an pastor-elder of college and young adults at Grace Bible Fellowship in Sunnyvale, California and professor of theology at the Cornerstone Bible College and Seminary in Vallejo, California.

SCOTT DENNY is the pastor overseeing biblical counseling and community group ministries at Grace Bible Church in Pleasant Hill, California.

RYAN RIPPEE is professor of church history and theology at The Cornerstone Bible College and Seminary in Vallejo, California.

www.ingramcontent.com/pod-product-compliance
Lightning Source LLC
Chambersburg PA
CBHW031446040426
42444CB00007B/998